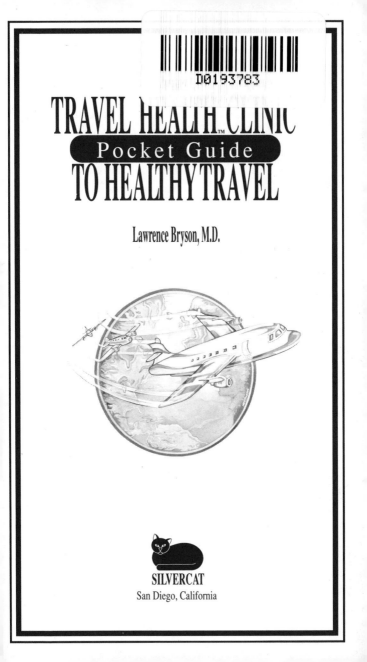

TRAVEL HEALTH™ CLINIC
Pocket Guide
TO HEALTHY TRAVEL

Lawrence Bryson, M.D.

SILVERCAT

San Diego, California

Package and cover design by Rick Covell,
Sausalito, California.

10 9 8 7 6 5 4 3 2

Library of Congress Cataloging-in-Publication Data

Bryson, Lawrence, 1943-

    The travel health clinic pocket guide to healthy travel / by Lawrence Bryson.

        p. cm.

    Includes index.

    ISBN 0-9624945-4-2 : $13.95

    1. Travel—Health aspects—Handbooks, manuals, etc. I. Title.

RA783.5.B79   1994   93-36906

613.6'8—dc20   CIP

Printed in the United States of America

To my wife,

Pattie,

without whose love,
patience, and professional
assistance as a nurse,
this book would still be
just a dream.

Contents

List of Sidebars

Introduction

Travel medicine is a new medical specialty addressing the needs of travelers. Its goals are to help travelers prevent illness and to help them receive appropriate and effective medical care if they do become ill.

As a specialist in travel medicine, I have had patients ask me repeatedly for a handy, readable pocket reference on travel health which they could consult before and during their trips. They have wanted practical, useful answers to questions about protecting themselves from the health hazards they encounter in their travels; about dealing with the health problems that arise; and about recognizing when they need to seek professional help.

The Travel Health™ *Clinic Pocket Guide To Healthy Travel* provides these answers in simple, nontechnical language, both for the traveler staying on traditional tourist routes and for the traveler venturing into remote areas where the amenities of modern civilization are unknown. It is a product, in part, of my own experiences and observations as a frequent traveler. It is even more a product of the experiences of so many of my patients, whose many fortunes and occasional misfortunes have contributed anonymously to this book.

Knowing how to minimize the health risks to which your travel exposes you can make the difference between an exciting and pleasurable trip and a frightening and costly experience. *The Travel Health*™ *Clinic Pocket Guide To Healthy Travel* will help you maximize your satisfaction and minimize your anxiety.

Healthy traveling begins long before the plane takes off or the boat embarks. Simple pre-departure planning can make the difference between a pleasant, memorable trip and a troubled, disappointing ordeal.

Once your trip has begun, taking a few easy, common-sense precautions can help keep you and your companions well even when others around you are suffering and uncomfortable.

Unfortunately, not even the best preparations work all the time. Sometimes, in spite of all your precautions, discomfort or sickness interrupts your trip. Knowing what to do at these times can help salvage both your trip and your peace of mind.

Finally, whether you became ill during your trip or experienced no travel-related health problems at all, a few simple, post-trip steps can ensure years of happy reminiscing.

The Travel Health™ Clinic Pocket Guide To Healthy Travel is a convenient and friendly reference for you to use both before you depart and during your trip, when other information may not be immediately available. It contains checklists, forms and worksheets, illustrations, advice, and information, all of which will help you stay a healthy traveler.

How To Use This Book

Glance through the chapters and the Table of Contents to become familiar with the way the book is organized. Photocopy the forms and worksheets in Appendix A—you have permission to make copies for your personal use. (As a service to readers, the publisher of this book will send you full-sized, reproducible copies of these forms for your use. Use the order form on the last page of this book to send for the *Forms Package* the checklists and worksheets contained in this book.)

Use these forms. Store the completed forms in one of the bound-in folders and carry them with you on your travels. They provide you with an instant record of where you have gone, what you have done, and what you have packed.

Read through all of Chapter 1, "Before You Depart," while you are still making your travel plans. It offers guidelines to help you plan for a healthy trip. It also gives you information about the immunizations you may need to receive and offers advice about other steps you can take to safeguard your health. Don't visit your doctor for your pre-trip check-up until you have read this chapter. It contains valuable information to help you ask important questions of your doctor. Chapter 1 will also help you put together an emergency medical kit to carry with you.

While you are packing, read Chapter 2, "Health Precautions for Travelers." This chapter identifies a number of precautions for preventing illness and discomfort during your trip. It may remind you of additional items to pack for your particular destinations. It will also prepare you for the preventive steps you can take at your destinations and give you a good idea of what to expect once your travels have begun.

Skim or read Chapter 3, "Treating Common Health Problems," and Chapter 4, "Getting Medical Help Abroad," so you will know where to find this information in case you need it. Chapter 3 will help you deal with minor ailments as they arise and help you recognize when you need to get medical help. Chapter 4 discusses how to find professional help when you need it. Even though you will probably never have to use this information, it is far preferable to know where it can be found than to waste valuable time looking for it during an emergency.

Even after a successful trip, there is always a chance that you have brought home more than souvenirs and photographs. Read Chapter 5, "After You Return," which discusses what you can do after you get home to make sure that the aftermath of your trip is a healthy one.

Also, look over the appendices. They contain forms, worksheets, and information you will find useful at each stage of your preparations and travels. In addition to a list of the addresses and phone numbers of American and Canadian embassies in a large number of popular and not-so-popular destinations, you will find a compilation of foreign phrases which will help you find medical assistance where English is not widely spoken. Other appendices describe some of the diseases, along with their immunizations, symptoms, and treatments, which may afflict international travelers. These will help you both prevent serious illness and recognize when you need to receive medical treatment abroad, and they will help you understand exactly what you are being vaccinated or treated for.

Finally, use the convenient, folders which are bound into the front and back covers of this book to help your organize and store the medical documents and other papers you'll be carrying. Put your records and papers in these folders. Pack this book, along with all your documents, in your carry-on luggage or put it in your pocket. In the event that you need information or papers, you will find them at your fingertips and not in the top drawer of your dresser in the hotel room or at the bottom of the big, blue two-suiter in the baggage compartment.

And, finally, have many wonderful, safe, and healthy trips!

An Important Message

The Travel Health™ Clinic Pocket Guide To Healthy Travel contains a number of generalizations which are accurate for most people most of the time. However, there is a limit to what any single book can do. A book can never anticipate every eventuality or substitute for the professional judgment that comes from years of medical training and experience.

This book will help you identify likely conditions when you are unable to obtain medical advice. It is not intended to help you diagnose medical conditions except when you have no alternative. An inaccurate self-diagnosis can be dangerous. Symptoms are flags which point to possible conditions. A number of diseases may share the same symptoms, so it is impossible to list symptoms in such a way as to eliminate all but the correct illness.

The symptoms which are listed here are the most common ways in which a disease or ailment may manifest itself. However, it would be impossible to list all the symptoms of any particular condition. Medical diagnosis is as much an art as it is a science, and it often requires the use of both sophisticated technology and intimate professional familiarity.

First aid and other treatment information is included to help you treat conditions during emergencies and at other times when a doctor is not available. This information, too, is presented as generalizations which are accurate in the majority of cases. But proper treatment cannot come from the pages of a book. It depends on an accurate diagnosis, an informed knowledge of the illness, and an attention to the needs and responses of the victim. Whenever possible, follow your doctor's recommended treatment. If you should have to treat yourself, consult with a doctor as soon as possible to ensure that your treatment is appropriate.

Drugs, medications, and dosages are listed for informational purposes only. Generic names are used in the text, for the most part, with trade names included as examples in parentheses. Except where indicated in the text, these medications should be safe for most people when taken in normal doses. However, many drugs have contraindications which restrict their use. While major contraindications are included when individual drugs are mentioned, it is impossible to list all contraindications. Self-medication can be dangerous. It is important to consult with a doctor before taking any drug, especially some of those which are available without prescription overseas.

This book should help you decide what to do in times of emergency when you are not able to get professional medical care. But medical diagnosis and treatment are far too complex to be condensed into single sentences and paragraphs. Accordingly, you should never use this or any book in place of a visit to the doctor.

Always consult a doctor whenever a health problem requires professional advice and care. Even if you believe that you have correctly diagnosed and treated a condition, a consultation with a doctor is still a good idea. Getting medical help when you don't need it is far preferable to failing to seek medical assistance when you do.

Chapter 1

Before You Depart

Your health planning should start at least four to six weeks before your scheduled departure. However, if you will be traveling for a month or more or going to a rural or undeveloped area of a country with a high health risk, allow an additional month or two for completing the necessary immunizations and other important arrangements.

How to Organize Your Planning

The *Trip Planning Checklist* (in Appendix A and in the forms package) will help you prepare for your trip. Make as many notes as you need to on this form during your preparations. The lead-times recommended on the checklist represent the approximate maximum times prior to departure to allow for each step. If you will be traveling only in low-risk areas, you may not need to allow as much time for some of the items, but it is always prudent to allow more time than you think is necessary.

Itinerary

Begin your health preparations by writing out your itinerary. This record will be invaluable when you and your doctor assess the health risks to which you will be exposed on your trip. Use the *Country Information Worksheet* in Appendix A to list the countries you will visit, the order in which you will visit them, the amount of time you plan to spend in each country, and the activities you plan to pursue while you are there. Pay attention to the risk levels (see below) in each of your destinations. Be sure to note whether you will be visiting areas off the normal tourist routes, where disease risks are greater. You will need all this information before you consult with your family physician and before you begin to assemble a medical kit to take with you on your travels. After you return home, the amount of medical follow-up you will need will be determined partly by the level of risk you were exposed to, the areas where you traveled, and the nature of your activities.

Levels of Health Risk

For practical purposes, the nations of the world can be divided into three groups representing three different degrees of health risk.

Risk Level I nations enjoy health standards comparable to those in the United States. Travel in these countries is no more risky to your health than traveling at home. Risk Level I countries include the United States and Canada, the nations of northern Europe including France, as well as Australia, New Zealand, and the urban parts of Japan. Barring special conditions or changes, you probably will not need to make any special health preparations for travel in these countries except to make sure your routine immunizations are up to date. A basic, Level I medical kit (discussed below) will probably be sufficient if you need to treat minor health problems or administer first aid. Your doctor or travel health clinic can advise you if special precautions will be necessary.

Risk Level II countries are those with health standards which are satisfactory but not equal to those of the United States. These nations include the European countries bordering the Mediterranean (except for France), the nations of Eastern Europe and the former Soviet Union, the Caribbean islands (except for Haiti and the Dominican Republic), Israel, South Africa, and rural Japan. In addition, Risk-Level II nations include some non-tropical parts of South America, some developed countries in Asia, and some Pacific islands.

In addition to the preparations you would make for travel to Risk Level I countries, you should also take precautions in Risk Level II countries against food- and water-borne illnesses. Except in some urban areas, you should stay away from tap water, using only bottled beverages or beverages made with boiled water and avoiding ice cubes made from tap water. You should also avoid undercooked or raw seafood, meat, and food from street vendors. A Level II medical kit will include water purification tablets along with simple medications for treating traveler's diarrhea. Depending on the destination, other precautions may be called for. Your doctor will help you assemble a medical kit appropriate for your Risk Level II destination.

Risk Level III countries are those where health risk are high and standards of sanitation and hygiene are poor or unpredictable. This group includes all of Central America and tropical South America, Mexico, Haiti, the Dominican Republic, and all the nations of Asia and Africa except for Japan, Israel, South Africa, and a few others. Besides the risks associated with Risk Level II nations, countries at Risk Level III also present a significant threat from insect-borne disease and increased risks from contaminated food and drinking water. Fresh-water lakes and streams in these countries may also expose travelers to the parasitic snail that causes schistosomiasis (see Appendix E).

Beyond the protective measures described for Risk Level I and II countries, Risk Level III precautions may include steps to protect against yellow fever, cholera, typhoid fever, and perhaps hepatitis. You will probably need to take anti-malaria medications, as well. Follow food, water, and hygiene precautions conscientiously, protect against insect bites, and avoid exposure to fresh-water lakes and streams. Your Risk Level III medical kit will be much more elaborate, possibly including prescription drugs. It should also contain emergency medical supplies if you expect to visit areas where medical care is not readily available. Carry a sheet sack to Risk Level III nations. This will create a physical barrier between you and your sleeping accommodations and help protect you from insect infestation.

The country listings in Appendix B include current risk levels. For general guidance on health preparations, consult this reference as you make detailed plans for your trip. Remember, though, that these estimates of risk levels are not necessarily precise. Risk levels are generalizations which are subject to change and revision depending on the times and the circumstances. Rural areas in Risk Level II, for example, may present Level III risks, while some urban areas in Level III countries may meet Level II or even Level I health standards. Likewise, nations with a given risk level today may experience political, economic, or other changes which affect their risk levels. For these reasons, it is important to consult with your doctor or travel health clinic while you are planning your trip.

In making your health preparations, plan for the most extreme health risks that you will encounter. If you will be traveling mainly in Risk Level II countries but plan to visit one Risk Level III country, for example, you may need to take precautions against malaria and begin your antimalaria regimen before you enter the Risk Level III area. Ask your doctor or travel health clinic for specific guidelines.

Also consider whether you will be traveling off the normal tourist routes. If you will be staying on principal tourist routes and living in tourist-class hotels, you will run less risk, even in Risk Level III countries, than you would if you were visiting rural areas and coming into close contact with local inhabitants or livestock. If you are an adventure traveler, such as a trekker or a river rafter, your trip will involve added risks. You may need extra immunizations and extra medical supplies in case you have a problem while far from medical help. Taking courses in first-aid and CPR is also a good idea if you plan to visit remote areas.

Medical and Dental Preparations

Six weeks or more before your departure, visit your family doctor for a checkup and a detailed discussion of your travel plans and inoculations. Bring your detailed itinerary to this appointment. Expect to have a routine exam and an evaluation of any chronic medical problems. Your doctor may recommend additional special procedures such as a tuberculosis skin test, a chest x-ray, an EKG, or a Pap smear (for women). If you will be carrying hypodermic needles or other medical devices, make sure you review proper usage and techniques with your doctor. Depending on the entry requirements of the countries on your itinerary, you may also need AIDS antibody testing. Ask your doctor about special precautions if you have any existing medical conditions.

Don't forget your dentist. A dental emergency can ruin a trip just as easily as illness. Visit your dentist for a checkup before your departure, allowing enough time for any necessary repairs.

Ask your doctor for written copies of all your prescriptions. Include these among the medical papers you take with you. Before you leave, obtain a sufficient supply of all your usual medications to last the entire trip, with enough extra to cover unexpected travel delays. Keep these medications in their original, labeled containers. If you wear glasses or contact lenses, get an extra pair and a copy of your lens prescription in case of loss or damage.

Have your doctor write a signed letter on his letterhead, summarizing your medical history and the medications you are taking, including the generic names of the drugs, the dosages, and the reason(s) you are taking them. This will help you avoid problems at customs. Your medical history should note if you have any allergies to medicines or other substances, and it should describe the symptoms produced by your allergic reactions. Make several copies of this medical history. Passport-sized copies of your medical history can be obtained by sending a copy of the history to **Medical Passport Foundation Inc.**, P.O. Box 820, Deland, FL 32721 (904-734-0639).

Be sure to add your doctor's name, address, and 24-hour phone number to the *Medical Information Checklist* and carry it with you when you travel.

If you have a serious medical problem, you can wear an identifying bracelet or tag describing the condition. These are available from **MedicAlert Foundation International**, P.O. Box 1009, Turlock, CA 95381 (209-668-3333) or (800-344-3226).

MedicAlert has a 24-hour phone service (209-634-4917) for emergency medical information.

Again, consider taking first-aid and CPR courses if you plan to visit remote areas where emergency medical care will not be readily available.

Sources of Health Information

Your family doctor will be able to answer most of your questions and administer most (if not all) of the immunizations you will need. But you may also want to get specialized advice from a travel health clinic about immunization and other health concerns, such as the health risks in various locations, the treatment of illnesses you may encounter in your travels, and special precautions which might be appropriate for your own health concerns. Travel health clinics can be located through your local medical society or in the yellow pages under "Physicians — Travel Medicine."

My own clinic—**Travel Health**™, 450 Sutter Street, San Francisco, CA 94108 (415-362-7177)—is one example of a full-service travel health facility. Travel Health™ is a one-stop travel medicine facility specializing in all aspects of travel medicine for private and corporate travelers. It offers immunizations, medicines, up-to-date CDC immunization recommendations for all countries, a twenty-four hour hotline for State Department travel advisories, and travel consultation and education services. A fully stocked travel-medicine pharmacy is on-site.

Up-to-the-minute information on immunization requirements and health precautions for international travel is available from the **Centers for Disease Control** (CDC) of the U.S. Public Health Service. The CDC's telephone information hotline provides information and advisories about vaccinations, food and water precautions, AIDS and foreign travel, disease outbreaks throughout the world, and disease risks and prevention in specific geographic areas, as well as CDC publications for international travelers. The number of the 24-hour hotline in Atlanta, Georgia is (404-332-4559). Using a touch-tone phone, callers can select specific information from a menu of options. Have a pencil and paper handy. If you are not calling from a touch-tone phone, an operator will come on the line during business hours and provide personal assistance.

A number of other information resources can enhance your travel knowledge. Magazines and periodicals dedicated to travel, the travel sections and columns of local newspapers, literature distributed by travel agents and tour agencies, all contain information which can be used while planning a healthy trip. Growing numbers of libraries, bookstores, and specialized travel stores offer titles which address the health and other concerns of travelers. No book or article—not even this book—can replace up-to-the-minute medical knowledge, but these books and articles frequently discuss hotels and restaurants, transportation, local culture and customs, language barriers, and other subjects which can affect your health and safety.

Computerized data services also offer useful information. For example, subscribers to CompuServe can obtain current information about almost every possible destination by looking up the current Worldwide Travel Advisories issued by the U.S. Department of State. In combination with the CDC hotline, this service can provide you with important information, not just about the medical care available in each nation, but also about the politics and culture of the countries you'll be visiting. In addition, it includes up-to-date addresses and phone numbers of Embassies and Consulates, both at home and at your destinations.

Immunizations

From your itinerary, your doctor will determine the immunizations you'll need both to safeguard your health during your trip and to comply with the entry requirements of the countries you will visit. You probably will not require special immunizations if you are traveling only to Risk Level I countries, but your doctor or travel health clinic should be consulted nevertheless.

Some immunizations require a series of injections over several weeks, so begin your planning early. Long lead time also minimizes the discomfort associated with multiple immunizations. If your departure time does not allow for a full series of immunizations, your doctor may be able to provide adequate protection from an abbreviated schedule. Appendix C, "Immunizations for Travelers," discusses the nature and scheduling requirements of some of the immunizations which travelers may need to receive.

Immunization Requirements

Current information on immunization requirements is available from the CDC Traveler's Hotline (404-332-4559). It can also be found in the publication, *Health Information for International Travelers*, issued by the U.S. Public Health Service, Division of Quarantine, Centers for Disease Control, Atlanta, GA 30333. This information is updated biweekly in another CDC publication, *Summary of Health Information for International Travel*. Your family physician or travel clinic will probably have copies of these publications. Private organizations such as the **International Association for Medical Assistance to Travelers** (716-754-4883; see page 29) also provide information on immunization requirements. A number of computerized databases are available by subscription to physicians and travel clinics. One of these, **Immunization Alert**, P. O. Box 406, Storrs, CT 06268 (203-487-0611), provides reports on selected countries to individual consumers on a one-time fee basis.

All immunizations should be recorded on an International Certificate of Vaccination, the 'yellow card' approved by the World Health Organization (WHO). This form is available from state and local health departments, travel clinics, and some private physicians. This certificate should be kept with your passport. Your physician or travel health clinic will use an official stamp to validate your required vaccinations. Immigration officials in some countries may bar your entry or force you to be vaccinated on the spot, under less than ideal conditions, if you do not have the required proof of vaccination.

Consult with your doctor about your immunizations. Some vaccinations, such as those prepared from live viruses, may present health hazards to certain people. If your doctor judges that a medical condition such as pregnancy or immune problems precludes your receiving a required immunization, have your doctor sign and date a letter explaining the medical reason for deferring this immunization. Your doctor should then validate this letter with an official stamp. Carry several copies in case you need to leave one with immigration officials.

Understanding the purpose and limitations of various immunizations will help you discuss your immunization needs with your doctor. There are three general categories of immunization: those that are routine for people living in developed countries; those that are required for entry into specific countries; and those that are recommended for travel in high-risk areas.

Routine Immunizations

These immunizations are easy to overlook, because people living in the industrialized world (Risk Level I) routinely receive them, usually during childhood. But the diseases against which they protect are still serious problems in many developing countries. Before you travel to Risk Level II or III areas, make sure that you have received these immunizations. Get boosters if your doctor or clinic recommends them.

Tetanus and Diphtheria: A booster is currently recommended every ten years.

Polio (Poliomyelitis): If you have already been immunized against polio, your doctor may recommend a booster. Otherwise, your doctor may suggest that you get a complete series of immunizations, or as many as practical, before traveling. The full series can take as long as a year to administer, so plan accordingly. Your doctor or travel clinic will determine whether you should receive the oral or the injected vaccine. Some polio vaccine is made from live virusses, which may present hazards to pregnant women and people with compromised immune systems.

Measles, Mumps, and Rubella: Measles has been greatly reduced in the United States, but it is still a major threat in developing countries. Anyone born after 1957 should consider receiving measles and mumps immunizations if they have not already had the diseases or been immunized. Because measles and mumps are both live vaccines, they should not normally be given to pregnant women or people with immune problems. Your doctor will probably recommend the Rubella (German measles) vaccine for children and adolescents as well as women of childbearing age who have not had the disease (unless they are presently pregnant). It is probably not a good idea to receive the rubella vaccine if you have a fever, which can increase the risk of side-effects.

Influenza: Most travelers can receive influenza immunization. Flu vaccine should especially be given to adults over sixty-five and people with serious chronic illnesses that place them at increased risk from influenza. Pregnant women traveling to areas of flu outbreaks should also consider receiving flu vaccine if they are beyond the first trimester of pregnancy.

Pneumococcus: Pneumococcal vaccine is usually recommended for travelers over sixty-five years of age, and for others at increased risk from pneumococcal infection, including people with chronic lung, liver, or heart disease, sickle-cell anemia, or non-functioning or surgically removed spleens.

Haemophilus: This vaccine provides protection against the most common cause of bacterial meningitis in the United States. A single dose of vaccine may be recommended for all children between the ages of eighteen months and five years, whether they are traveling or not.

Required Immunizations

Only immunizations against cholera and yellow fever are presently required for entry into certain countries. At one time, smallpox immunization was also required, but smallpox has been declared eradicated worldwide since 1980, and, as of this writing, no country requires smallpox vaccination for entry.

Cholera: This intestinal infection is acquired primarily from contaminated food and water. The vaccine is not completely effective, and even when it works, protection lasts for only five to six months. The best protection against this disease is to take proper precautions with the food and water you consume (see pages 43-46). Still, some countries require proof of cholera vaccination for all in-coming travelers, while others require it for those arriving from countries where cholera infection is present. Consult up-to-date information for the countries you will be visiting to see whether you will need to receive this vaccination. If it will be required, your doctor or travel health clinic can administer the vaccination and record it on your immunization certificate.

If you are getting a cholera vaccination simply to satisfy entry requirements, a single injection seven days prior to entry will probably suffice. However, if you will be spending long periods in areas of cholera outbreak or if you will be living in extremely unsanitary conditions in Risk Level III areas, consider receiving a regular series of cholera vaccine (currently two injections), even if the immunization is not required.

If you are pregnant or if you have had a previous allergic reaction to cholera vaccine, your doctor will probably recommend against your having this vaccination. If you still plan to visit countries requiring cholera vaccination, carry an officially stamped letter from your physician explaining the reason why the vaccination was not administered.

Yellow fever: The vaccine against this mosquito-transmitted virus is very effective, lasts for 10 years, and is appropriate for almost everyone traveling where yellow fever is a risk—primarily the tropical regions of Africa and the Americas. This vaccine should normally not be given to infants under nine months of age, pregnant women, people with reduced immunity, or people with egg allergy (because the vaccine may be prepared in eggs). Travelers who cannot receive yellow fever vaccine should carry a doctor's letter explaining the medical reason if they will be visiting countries requiring this vaccination.

Yellow fever vaccine is presently administered only by designated vaccination centers. Your doctor, travel clinic, or local health department can arrange for you to receive this vaccination if you will need it.

Recommended Immunizations for Travel in High-Risk Areas

Your doctor or travel health clinic may recommend other vaccinations as well, depending on your itinerary, your intended activities, and the prevailing conditions at the time of your trip. These recommended immunizations may include one or more of the following:

Hepatitis A: This viral disease of the liver is transmitted in food and water which has been contaminated by feces. Immune globulin (gamma globulin) provides protection against Hepatitis A for three to six months, depending on the dose received. It is normally recommended for travelers who will be spending time in areas where sanitation standards are questionable.

Hepatitis B: Hepatitis B is more serious than Hepatitis A. Health workers and others who will be in prolonged contact with blood and other body fluids in areas where hepatitis is widespread should consider receiving the vaccination. It may also be recommended for people who anticipate sexual contact with local residents in these areas.

Japanese encephalitis: This viral inflammation is carried by mosquitos in Asia during the summer and fall months. It produces flu-like symptoms and can be fatal. A new vaccine is now available. Ask your doctor or travel health clinic about it if you are going to be traveling where the disease is a hazard.

Meningococcal meningitis: This vaccination may be recommended for people who are going to areas where large epidemics have been reported. In recent years, epidemics have occurred in Nepal, sub-Saharan Africa, and New Delhi in India. Consult your doctor if you are traveling with children. This vaccine may not be fully effective in children under the age of two, so young children should be taken to areas of epidemic only with extreme caution.

If you will be living or working in remote Risk Level III areas for extended periods of time, you should also talk with your doctor about the following additional immunizations:

Plague: A vaccine against bubonic plague may be recommended for people who will come into contact with animals carrying the fleas which transmit this infamous disease. Immunization is fairly uncommon, normally prescribed only for those traveling to areas where plague is endemic. Pregnant women, however, should not normally receive a plague vaccination. The CDC hotline (404-332-4559) can provide you and your doctor with up-to-the-minute information about the presence of plague at your destination.

Rabies: This vaccine may be especially advisable if you anticipate contact with animals. Even with the vaccination, you will probably need to receive immediate treatment with a series of rabies shots if you are bitten by an infected animal. However, the initial vaccination will reduce the complications which can be associated with post-exposure treatment.

Typhoid Fever: Immunization against typhoid is generally recommended for people who will be staying for long periods in areas where food and water may be contaminated. Pregnant women should talk to their doctors before receiving typhoid vaccine, which can harm the fetus. Injectable typhoid vaccine, which can cause fever and slight pain at the site of injection, is only moderately effective and lasts only one to three years. An oral vaccine, now available in the United States, works just as well and has fewer side effects. Your doctor will probably begin your oral vaccine regimen at least two weeks before your departure.

Tuberculosis Skin Test

An additional precaution for travelers to Risk Level II and III areas is a Tuberculosis skin test. Tuberculosis (TB) is not a common illness among travelers, but it can be a risk to those with prolonged exposure to local people who have the disease. A skin test before you depart will determine whether you have been exposed in the past. If your pre-trip test was negative and your retest three to four weeks after your return is positive, your doctor will treat you with appropriate medication.

Malaria Protection

In addition to your immunizations, determine from your doctor, your travel clinic, or the CDC Hotline (404-332-4559) if you will be traveling where exposure to malaria is possible. Malaria is the foremost infectious disease in the world today, and its dangers to travelers, especially in the tropics, are increasing. By far, most travelers who become ill with malaria have failed to take medications to protect against the disease.

Malaria can be a very dangerous illness if untreated. One form can be deadly. It is transmitted by the bite of a mosquito infected with a parasite. The mosquito bites mainly at dusk and after dark. Avoiding mosquito bites is a crucial element of protecting against malaria (see "Insect Protection" in Chapter 2). Symptoms of infection may appear from one week to months after exposure. Once symptoms do appear, the disease takes hold rapidly. It is marked by chills, fever, and headache, followed by sweating. The symptoms subside and then recur within days.

Antimalaria Drugs

Antimalaria drugs are prescribed to minimize the risk of infection, but they do not eliminate it completely. In fact, at present, no drug fully protects against malaria infection. Your doctor will normally instruct you to begin taking most antimalaria drugs one or two weeks before traveling to a malarious area. This regimen builds up protective levels of the drug in your blood and, if your schedule permits, allows your doctor to watch for side effects while you are still at home. Your doctor will probably recommend that you take the medication according to a prescribed schedule—generally once a week, always on the same day—while you are traveling in malaria areas and to continue for at least four additional weeks after leaving areas of potential exposure.

The specific antimalaria drugs you use, as well as your schedule of use, will depend on your destination and the length of your stay. Your physician will build an antimalaria regimen that suits your travel plans and your medical status. It will probably involve one of the following drugs.

The preferred antimalaria medication as of this writing is chloroquine (Aralen®) which has a history of relatively safe and effective use. Normally taken in 500 mg. doses once a week, chloroquine is generally effective against malaria in Central America west of the

Canal Zone, in Mexico, Haiti, the Dominican Republic, and in most of the Middle East (including Egypt).

Unfortunately, chloroquine-resistant strains of malaria have appeared in many parts of the world, making the use of other drugs necessary. All these other drugs have potential drawbacks. For travel to these malarious areas, the current drug of choice is mefloquine (Lariam®), in doses of 250 mg. taken once a week. Though highly effective, it does present risks for some travelers (see below). Moreover, mefloquine may be difficult to obtain because its supply is limited.

For people unable to take mefloquine, alternative drug regimens are available for travel to areas of chloroquine resistance. If your risk of exposure to malaria (i.e., exposure to nighttime mosquito bites) will be relatively low, your doctor may direct you to take a weekly dose of chloroquine and to carry a standby supply of pyrimethamine sulfadoxide (Fansidar®)for use in prescribed amounts at any sign of fever or other malarial symptom. At one time, Fansidar® was the usual treatment for chloroquine-resistant strains of malaria. However, Fansidar® has a number of potentially serious side effects and is no longer effective against all chloroquine-resistant strains. Fansidar® should be considered a temporary measure until professional medical help can be obtained.

A second alternative to mefloquine is 100 mg. of doxycycline (such as Vibramycin®) daily. Prevention with doxycycline usually begins one to two days prior to entering the malarious area, continuing for the duration of the stay and for four weeks following departure. Doxycline is an alternative for travelers who cannot take Fansidar®, for those who are at relatively high risk for malaria exposure, or for anyone else traveling in areas of Fansidar® resistance.

Patterns of malaria risk and drug resistance are constantly changing. Travel health clinics or the CDC Hotline (404-332-4559) can provide up-to-date advice on disease risk and on the most effective antimalaria medication for each area.

Cautions Concerning Antimalaria Drugs

Antimalarial drugs should only be taken with your doctor's approval. Chloroquine is relatively safe for most people. Taking it after meals may help to reduce any minor side effects. Other antimalaria drugs may present greater risks. Mefloquine should not be taken by small children, by pregnant or lactating women, or by people with cardiac, seizure, or psychiatric disorders. It can interact dangerously with certain cardiac and anti-seizure medications. Fansidar® has been known to produce severe and sometimes fatal skin reactions, and it cannot be taken by certain people, including those allergic to sulfa drugs. Doxycycline produces many of the side-effects associated with tetracycline. It may cause photosensitivity reactions which necessitate special precautions against sun exposure, and it can promote vaginal yeast infections in women.

Children usually can be safely treated with chloroquine, although your doctor should be consulted about the proper child's dose. It has a very bitter taste and may be more acceptable to children if mixed with food or drink. Mefloquine, doxycycline, and Fansidar® all have restrictions governing their use by children. Your doctor will advise you about which drug is appropriate for your child.

Pregnant women are at particular risk from malaria and should consult with their physicians before traveling to areas of malaria infection. At this time, chloroquine is considered relatively safe for pregnant women to take, but mefloquine and Fansidar® should not be taken during pregnancy. The best advice for pregnant women would be to avoid areas where chloroquine-resistant strains of malaria are present. If you have to travel into these areas, check with your doctor or travel clinic for recommendations on safe malaria protection.

Other drugs are also available for protecting against malaria. Consult your travel health specialist to discuss the options. Some antimalaria drugs are not available in the United Status but are sold in other countries. These drugs may present hazards. Get reliable medical advice before taking these or any other drugs which you did not bring from home.

Some forms of malaria can stay in the liver and cause relapses for years. If you should have a reappearance of malaria symptoms after returning home, contact your doctor for appropriate medication to prevent further relapses.

Finally, if you have taken anti-malarial drugs and traveled in a malaria-infested area, you will not be able to donate blood for a period of at least three years.

Preventing Travelers Diarrhea

By far the most common illness to plague travelers, especially in developing countries, is traveler's diarrhea. This uncomfortable problem is characterized by frequent, unformed stools which are often accompanied by cramps. It is slightly more common among young adults than among older people. Traveler's diarrhea is caused by strains of intestinal bacteria which contaminate food and water in areas with poor sanitation. The problem generally goes away on its own in a few days with proper replacement of the fluids lost in the stools.

The best protection against traveler's diarrhea is to be scrupulous in observing the food and water precautions described in the next chapter. Travelers to Risk Level II or III countries should include water purification tablets and an immersion coil for boiling water in their medical kits. Be prepared to purify water by boiling and/or chemical disinfection wherever there is no reliable supply of safe drinking water.

Some drugs, including the antibiotics doxycycline and TMP/SMZ (such as Bactrim®) or Cipro®, and large doses of a bismuth subsalicylate like Pepto-Bismol® are capable of preventing many cases of traveler's diarrhea. However, the potentially harmful effects of taking these drugs preventively, consuming large doses over a long period of time, far outweigh the possible benefits of avoiding a relatively mild infirmity. If you have a medical condition which makes diarrhea a serious concern, your doctor may be able to prescribe anti-diarrhea drugs which are tailored to your needs.

For most people, the greatest danger from diarrhea is dehydration. This usually can be treated with oral rehydration drinks. Include packets of Oral Rehydration Formula (see Sidebar 3B, pages 65-66) in your medical kit if you will be traveling in Risk Level III areas. Your doctor may also recommend that you carry Pepto-Bismol® or other medication for treating diarrhea. Some people, including pregnant women, young children, and persons taking blood-thinning drugs, may not be able to take these medicines, so they must be especially careful to avoid contaminated food and water.

Arranging for Medical Help Abroad

Leave a copy of your travel itinerary, your medical history, other important papers, and the name, address, and phone number of your family doctor with a responsible person at home. The *Emergency Information Checklist* in Appendix A will help you assemble the important information. Carry a photocopy of this worksheet with you so you know exactly what information your contact has. Ask him or her to accept an international collect phone call in case of emergency. Be sure to bring the contact person's phone number and address with you on your trip.

English-Speaking Doctors

The best time to find out about emergency medical care and English-speaking doctors at your destinations is *before* you leave. This information should be copied to your *Country Information Worksheet*. A good resource is the *Directory* of English-speaking doctors published by the **International Association for Medical Assistance to Travelers** (IAMAT), 417 Center Street, Lewiston, NY 14092 (716-754-4883). Membership is free, but a donation is requested. IAMAT supplies its members with an international, city-by-city list of English-speaking doctors, all of whom follow a consistent and very reasonable fee schedule. The association also provides information on disease risks, climate conditions, and immunization requirements for specific destinations. In addition, IAMAT makes packages of oral rehydration solution available.

Another source of referrals to English-speaking doctors is **International SOS Assistance**, Box 11568, Philadelphia, PA 19116 (215-245-4707 or 800-523-8930). A membership fee is required, and there is no fixed fee schedule for participating physicians. The organization provides a variety of services for travelers, including medical evacuation and repatriation.

Embassies

American and Canadian Embassies can be very helpful if you have a medical emergency. They can direct you to English-speaking doctors and other medical facilities in addition to providing essential diplomatic services. Appendix B includes a country-by-country list of embassy addresses and phone numbers. Record this information for each country you plan to visit on the *Country Information Worksheet*.

Traveler's Insurance

If you have health insurance, determine what—and if—it will pay for medical care administered outside of the United States. Even if your insurance does provide coverage, it will probably include restrictions. You may need to consider supplemental insurance. Blue Cross and Blue Shield, for example, cover some foreign medical treatment, but only on a reimbursement basis. Medicare and Medicaid, on the other hand, do not reimburse for health expenses outside the country. Some supplemental policies for Medicare patients, such as those offered through the **American Association of Retired Persons** (AARP), will cover medical care received outside the United States.

A number of insurance companies offer special policies for travelers. Your travel or insurance agent can provide referrals. Major credit card companies generally offer travel insurance to card holders. Traveler's insurance covers many costly emergency situations, such as medical evacuation, which can cost tens of thousands of dollars. The cost is usually reasonable for very comprehensive coverage. Evaluate any traveler's insurance policy carefully to be sure it provides the services you want.

Most traveler's insurance policies require that you pay at the time of treatment, to be reimbursed later. You will therefore need to have ready access to cash in a medical emergency, either through your credit card or through a wire transfer. The American Embassy can help you arrange a transfer of money from home. To facilitate reimbursement, bring some insurance claim forms with you and have them filled out in English at the time of treatment. You will need to be treated by licensed medical personnel.

Each policy includes its own clauses and conditions. Be sure to read your policy carefully to identify exactly what your policy will cover and any special conditions which could affect your responsiblities and your coverage.

Evacuation

You should also prepare an evacuation plan in the event of an illness or accident overseas. In rural or remote areas, you may need to arrange for transportation to an urban area where modern medical facilities exist. At other times, you may need to arrange for a return home.

Evacuation is never easy, especially when it has to be arranged during a crisis. Making an evacuation plan before you leave is simply prudent. Your insurance carrier and the State Department, as well as many of the travelers-aid organizations mentioned through the text, can give you information about evacuations from your specific destinations.

What to Pack

Medical Kits and Documents

Your medical kit should contain all the health and medical supplies you might need during your trip. What you pack will depend partly on where you are going, how long you will be gone, and whether you will be traveling off the established tourist routes in areas where medical care may not be readily available.

Use the *Medical Kit Checklist* in Appendix A to help prepare your personal medical kit. With your doctor's advice, customize it for your own needs and itinerary. What you put in your kit will vary according to the risk levels of the countries on your itinerary. You will need to prepare a kit which is appropriate for the greatest risks to which you will be exposed. Some travelers are not able to take certain of the over-the-counter medications recommended on the form, so review the medications with your doctor before including them in your kit. Fill any prescriptions you need and include these as well.

A thorough medical kit will also include appropriate medical documents. The *Medical Documents Checklist* (also in Appendix A) will help you select the records you should carry. Plan to carry all the routine papers, such as immunization certificates and copies of prescriptions. But you should also include papers which document your special medical conditions and those of others in your party.

Pack your medical supplies, medications, first-aid equipment, all of your medical documents, and this book in your carry-on luggage. This will insure that these essential items stay with you even if your primary luggage becomes lost.

Clothing

If you will be traveling in hot climates, emphasize loose-fitting, light-colored clothing (but not white, which shows dirt too easily). Cotton is an ideal fabric, as long as it is heavy enough to protect against mosquito bites where malaria is a danger. Wear comfortable, well broken-in shoes, and pack an adequate supply of absorbent socks to allow for daily changes. For sun protection bring sunglasses and a broad-brimmed hat. Find out about any local customs or expectations which might influence your selection of clothing, and dress accordingly. In some places, for example, women should not wear shorts or sleeveless shirts.

If your sleeping accommodations will expose you to the risk of insect infestation, pack a sheet sack. You can make one by sewing two sheets together at the sides into the form a sleeping bag. Or you can purchase a commercial sheet sack at camping, outdoors, surplus, or similar retail outlets.

For colder destinations, pack loose-fitting clothing which can be layered to regulate body heat. As temperatures fluctuate, these layers can be put on or removed as necessary to adjust your comfort and warmth. Wool is a good choice of cold weather fabric. Polypropylene 'long johns,' which wick perspiration away from the skin, are useful to prevent chilling. Bring a knit hat to preserve your body heat and gloves or mittens to protect your fingers.

Travelers with Special Concerns

Traveling with Young Children

Most young children, even infants, can travel safely to most destinations if plans are carefully made ahead of time. There are a few exceptions. Infants younger than a month probably should not fly. When younger than two weeks of age they are sensitive to the air-pressure changes experienced while flying. Infants under one month should not be exposed to crowds—even the crowds on an airplane—because their immune systems are not yet fully developed.

Pay special attention to immunizations and other preventive measures for children. If you are planning to travel with children, consult with your family doctor or pediatrician at least six weeks before your departure.

Breast feeding is the safest and most convenient way to feed infants when traveling in countries with poor sanitation and hygiene. However, the stress of travel or illness may interfere with the ability to produce milk, so infant formula should be brought along as well. Try out the formula before you leave to make sure that your infant will accept it. And if you do prepare formula overseas, always prepare it with water which you have purified.

Ask your pediatrician about the correct children's dosages for the medications in your medical kit. Children who have had prior ear infections or strep throat should be examined by a pediatrician, who may prescribe a supply of an antibiotic in case of problems on the trip.

You will need to add a few additional items to your medical kit when traveling with children. The *Medical Kit Checklist* includes a minimum list of additional items travelers with children should carry.

If it is appropriate, bring a sufficient number of disposable diapers, and ask your travel agent if more will be available at your destination. If there is any doubt, bring cloth diapers and rubber panties.

Your pediatrician or travel clinic will help you get the names of physicians who practice children's medicine at each of your destinations.

Have a dental checkup for your child at the same time you have one for yourself, allowing time for any necessary work to be done.

Take a supply of childproof locks and outlet covers. After you arrive at your destination, you can childproof your hotel room to guard against accidents.

Children are very susceptible to sunburn. Pack a sunscreen and be prepared to keep your child out of the hot midday sun.

Make sure to provide adequate fluid replacement to prevent dehydration if your child has diarrhea. Bring packets of Oral Rehydration Formula (Sidebar 3B, pages

65-66), especially if you will be traveling in Risk Level II and III areas. Because tetracycline discolors children's teeth, you should not normally use it on children without your doctor's approval. Instead, pack a bismuth subsalicylate like Pepto-Bismol®, which is safe for most children over the age of two.

Note: Aspirin has been associated with the development of Reye's Syndrome in children. Reye's Syndrome can be serious and sometimes fatal. Unless your doctor recommends otherwise, never give aspirin to children, or for that matter to anyone under the age of twenty. Acetaminophen has not been linked to this serious disorder and it should normally be administered instead.

If your child needs medical treatment abroad, make sure you understand what the treatment is. If you have any doubts as to its safety—or any questions whatsoever—call your pediatrician back home. Keep a careful record of the diagnosis and of any medications or treatments your child receives. Report them to your child's doctor immediately when your return home.

Traveling While Pregnant

If you are pregnant, make sure your obstetrician knows about your schedule and itinerary. The safest time to travel during pregnancy is during the second trimester. During the first three months, when the risks of complication are high, remote locations with poor sanitary standards should be avoided. During the last three months, premature labor is possible. Air travel may not be recommended after thirty-five weeks of pregnancy. Some airlines have restrictions on flying even earlier in pregnancy.

Because pregnant women should not receive certain immunizations (see "Immunizations," pages 16-22 above), you should get a signed letter from your doctor saying that these vaccines were withheld for medical reasons. Carry several copies of this letter in case you need to leave them with immigration officials.

Avoid all places where there is a high risk of exposure to diseases against which you cannot be immunized. In particular, you should stay away from areas where chloroquine-resistant strains of malaria are present, because the drugs used to protect against this serious form of the disease are not advisable during pregnancy. If possible, avoid destinations at altitudes above 6,000 feet, where you and your fetus will receive less oxygen.

Talk to your doctor about the warning signs of possible problems with a pregnancy, and obtain the name of a reliable obstetrician at each of your destinations. If you must travel during your last trimester, consider carrying a blood pressure monitor. This will inform you if your blood pressure becomes too low, a sign of potential problems for the fetus.

Traveler's diarrhea presents special problems for pregnant women, because treatment possibilities are much more limited. The high salicylate level in Pepto-Bismol® can cause bleeding, while doxycycline can harm the bones and teeth of the fetus during the last three months. Some of the newer diarrhea medications, such as Diasorb®, seem to be safe for pregnant women, but nothing works better than scrupulously observing the food and drink precautions discussed in the next chapter.

Elderly Travelers

Older adults can usually travel safely to most destinations as long as they remember that their reactions to environmental conditions may be more pronounced than those of younger travelers. For example, elderly people are more susceptible to sunburn, heat prostration, and heat stroke, and certain drugs may sensitize their skin to the sun. Older travelers should check with their physician about the possibility of adverse reactions to environmental, pharmacological, and other influences and about possible interactions between drugs and environmental influences.

Senior travelers are more prone to dehydration, so they should plan to drink plenty of additional liquids.

They are also more susceptible to injury from cold. Those taking tranquilizers or barbiturates are at increased risk, because they tend to feel the cold less and may not recognize their exposure as quickly.

Older people should travel to high altitudes more slowly and limit their activity between ascents. While walking, a cane or other aid can be used to prevent falls.

Extra immunizations and other precautions may also be appropriate for the older traveler. Your family doctor or travel clinic will advise you of any additional steps you can take to make your travels safer and healthier.

Handicapped Travelers

Travelers with impaired mobility can still travel with relative freedom. A few extra precautions are advisable, however, to make sure that your destinations offer proper access at airports, hotels, and other necessary facilities and services. A good source of information is *International Directory of Access Guides*, published by Rehabilitation International, 1123 Broadway, Suite 704, New York, New York 10010 (212-972-2707). Other dependable sources are the **Society for Advancement of Travel for the Handicapped**, 26 Court Street, Brooklyn NY 11242 (718-858-5483) and the **Information Center for Individuals with Disabilities**, 20 Park Plaza, Suite 330, Boston, MA 02116 (617-727-5540 or 800-462-5015).

Special Medical Problems

Even if you have a chronic medical problem such as heart disease or diabetes, you may still be able to travel safely as long as you make appropriate pre-trip preparations. Consult with your doctor about restrictions on your activities or the places you can visit, and adjust your travel plans accordingly. Ask your doctor or travel clinic for a list of doctors who are equipped to treat your special problems abroad.

Have your doctor write a signed letter on letterhead explaining your special medical problems and listing your medications with their generic names and the reasons you are taking them.

If you have special medical problems, you should wear an identifying tag or bracelet, such as one of those available from **MedicAlert Foundation International** (see page 14).

Heart Disease

If you suffer from heart disease, you should not travel unless your condition is stable. Even then, you should carry a copy of a recent electrocardiogram and know the warning signs of heart attack. Review your travel plans with your doctor and accept any restrictions he or she may impose. You may need to avoid high altitudes or limit the length of time you drive an automobile.

If you have an implanted pacemaker, have it checked before you leave. Your doctor should write a note saying that you have an implanted pacemaker, including the model and lot number, to avoid problems at airport security checkpoints. Have your doctor review your medical kit to make sure that it contains nothing that will interact harmfully with your regular prescription medications. If you are taking diuretics for heart problems or high blood pressure, be especially careful to avoid dehydration from heat or diarrhea.

Lung disease

Discuss your detailed travel plans with your physician to see if your condition rules out any destinations or activities. Ask if you can be exposed to high altitude and how much exercise you can tolerate.

Make sure supplemental oxygen will be available if there is a chance you will need it. Small, portable systems can be purchased where medical equipment and supplies are sold. Airlines will make oxygen available if your doctor requests it. In the event of an emergency abroad, the American or Canadian embassy can help you find a supply of oxygen.

Diabetes

If you are diabetic and use insulin, you will need to adjust your insulin dosage while traveling on long east-west flights over six or more time zones. Your doctor will tell you how to do this in view of your own specific needs. It is also important to monitor your blood sugar levels carefully and to observe other precautions for diabetic care scrupulously.

Your medical kit will need to include special diabetic supplies, including an adequate supply of insulin, syringes, and testing materials. Refrigerate your insulin as soon as you arrive at your destination. Avoid exposing insulin to high temperatures, such as those in the glove compartment or trunk of a car. Store insulin in an ice-filled cooler or thermos when traveling in hot places. Do not let insulin freeze in colder locations. Additional insulin will probably be available in most, but not all, parts of the world. If you should run out of insulin or supplies, contact a local specialist or the nearest foreign service outpost.

Immune problems

If your immune system is impaired by aging, AIDS, medications such as cortisone or chemotherapy, or other medical conditions, you have a higher risk of infectious disease. Consult with your doctor about the risks of traveling with compromised immunity and of receiving certain immunizations.

Immune-compromised individuals, who may not be able to fight off the infection from live inoculations, should not receive vaccines containing live organisms. To avoid problems on entering countries where these immunizations are required, have your doctor write a letter stating that you have not received these immunizations for medical reasons. Carry several copies of this letter.

Many countries now require proof of HIV antibody testing for certain categories of visitors. Some countries will not accept test results from the U.S., insisting instead that the testing be done on entry. If you are

HIV-positive or if you have AIDS or ARC, it will be difficult for you to enter some countries. The regulations are constantly changing. Consult with travel clinics, doctors who subscribe to computerized data bases or contact the consulates of countries you plan to visit for up-to-the-minute information on these restrictions.

Evaluating Cruises and Spas

When planning a cruise, make sure that the ships you are considering meet established standards of sanitation. To obtain a report on the most recent sanitary inspection of a specific vessel, contact **Chief of Vessel Sanitation Activity**, Center for Environmental Health and Injury Control, 1015 N. America Way, Room 107, Miami, FL 33132 (305-536-4307). Also ask the cruise line about the credentials of the ship's physician and about how medical emergencies are dealt with at sea.

If your foreign travel plans include a stay at a spa, ask the spa about its standards of hygiene. Take common-sense precautions. For example, do not make a reservation at any spa which does not sterilize instruments used for beauty treatments or otherwise maintain absolute cleanliness. If acupuncture treatments are offered, make sure that disposable needles are used or that permanent needles are sterilized before each treatment. Do not accept any spa treatments that present a possible health risk, such as injections of blood or cellular products which may be contaminated with HIV or other infectious organisms. Your doctor or travel health clinic will help you evaluate the health standards of the spas, cruise ships, or other attractions which you are considering.

Chapter 2

Health Precautions for Travelers

Once you are on your way, you will no longer have immediate access to familiar medical resources. You will need to rely on good judgment, common sense, and careful precautions to minimize health problems and to respond quickly and appropriately if problems do occur. Fortunately, most travel-related health problems are preventable. This chapter describes a number of precautions which can spare you much discomfort and give you confidence that you have control over your health even in unfamiliar surroundings. Remember, preventing problems is much easier than treating them.

Jet Lag

Modern jet planes can cross many time zones in a relatively short period of time. When you arrive at your destination, the body clock which regulates your sleep, wakefulness, and other activities may be disturbed. This disruption can produce irritability, fatigue, sleep difficulties, poor concentration, loss of appetite, and other discomforts. Jet lag is not a problem on north-south flights which do not cross time zones. And, it is generally easier to adjust to a time shift when traveling from east to west than from west to east.

A number of strategies have been developed to minimize jet lag. One of the simplest involves switching to the sleeping and eating schedule of your destination, either while in flight or immediately upon arrival. Unless you initiate this strategy before departure, however, it only reduces the length of time when jet lag is a problem. It does not prevent jet lag or lessen the initial discomfort.

Another approach adjusts the body clock with diet. The *Anti-Jet-Lag Diet*, developed by Dr. Charles F. Ehret of Argonne National Laboratories, alternates days of 'feasting' on high-protein breakfasts and lunches and high-carbohydrate dinners with days of 'fasting' on small, low-calorie meals. Start by feasting on the fourth day before arriving at your destination, then fast on the third day, feast on the second, and fast one day before. During the first three days, drink beverages which contain caffeine only between 3 and 5 PM. On the day before arrival, however, you should drink caffeine in the morning for a westbound flight or between 6 and 11PM for an eastbound flight. Do not drink alcohol on the plane. To obtain a wallet-sized card outlining this diet, send a stamped, self-addressed envelope to **Anti-Jet-Lag Diet**, OPA, Argonne National Laboratory, 9700 South Cass Ave., Argonne, IL 60439.

A third technique uses light to reset the body clock, because light has the ability to inhibit the production of a brain hormone that triggers sleep. If you are traveling from east to west and arrive during daylight, go outside and take a walk in the sun. If you are traveling from west to east, avoid the sun for the rest of the day. The next morning, no matter which direction you have traveled, take a walk outdoors in the sunshine. Avoid wearing sunglasses when outdoors during the first few days, and keep lights on indoors during the daytime.

A computerized service combines these strategies to provide travelers with instructions customized around their particular itineraries. For information, contact **Jet Ready**, Kinetic Software, Inc., 12672 Skyline Boulevard, Woodside, CA 94062 (415) 851-4484.

Although no anti-jet-lag protocol is completely effective, these techniques will help you minimize the inconvenience. All of these techniques will work better if you also:

- Exercise regularly during the two or three weeks before your departure to build up your resistance to fatigue.
- Schedule your flight so that you arrive in the late afternoon or evening and are not faced with a full day's activities.
- Get a good night's sleep the night before you travel.
- Take a nap on a long flight, preferably during the hours corresponding to nighttime at your destination.
- Don't smoke, drink alcohol, or take unnecessary medications during your flight.
- Get up and walk around during the flight.
- Drink plenty of fluids on the plane.

Diabetics take note: You will need help from your doctors in adjusting your insulin dosage to compensate for the change in time zones. See the section on diabetic travelers in Chapter 1 (page 36) for additional information.

Motion Sickness

Turbulent airplane flights, boat voyages, and bus or auto trips over bumpy, winding roads can all cause motion sickness. If you are susceptible to motion sickness, avoid alcohol as well as fried, fatty, and spicy foods before and during travel. Don't travel on an empty stomach, but eat small amounts of bland foods and drink plenty of non-alcoholic liquids. Choose a seat in the middle section of a boat or plane or in the front of a car or bus. Keep your eyes straight ahead, looking at the horizon. Recline or lie down if possible, and do not read.

The nonprescription antihistamines, dimenhydrinate (Dramamine®) and promethazine (Phenergan®), are often used to prevent motion sickness. Both are usually

taken thirty to sixty minutes before departure. Drama-
mine is typically repeated every four hours and Phener-
gan every twelve hours. A newer anti-motion-sickness
treatment, Transderm Scop®, is applied as a small patch
behind the ear, where it releases the drug scopolamine
through the skin for about three days. The patch is
attached two to four hours before traveling to give it
time to take effect.

*Check with your doctor before taking any of these
anti-motion-sickness drugs.* They are not advisable for
people with certain medical conditions. All these drugs
can cause drowsiness, so do not drive while you are
using them.

Once motion sickness has commenced, it is much more
difficult to treat. If you feel nauseous during your trip, eat
bland foods such as soda crackers. If possible, get some
fresh air—open the car window, go on deck on a cruise, or
turn on the air vent on an airplane. Don't smoke. Sit quietly
and relax. Eventually motion sickness will pass, although
eventually may seem like an eternity.

Hotel Safety

When you check into your hotel, familiarize yourself
with the exits, noting at least two escape routes in case
of fire. If a fire breaks out in your hotel and smoke fills
the air, get down on the floor. Before moving from one
room to another, feel the door. Do not open it if the door
is hot. If it is safe, open the door, go through on your
hands and knees, and follow one of your escape routes.

If you are trapped in your room, shut the doors and
open the windows. Soak towels and sheets in cold water
and stuff them into the crack of the door, ventilator
openings, and any other places where smoke might
come in. Your room phone may still work. If it does,
call the desk (or an outside emergency number) and give
the number of the room where you are trapped.

If you are traveling with a small child, make sure that
your hotel room presents no hazards to a curious young-
ster. For example, check for lamps or breakables that

might be pulled over. Make sure electric outlets are safely covered. Carry adhesive tape or cabinet locks to secure your medicines.

Food and Water Precautions

Food

Be especially careful about what you eat during the first few days in a new, foreign location. Your system will adjust gradually. Do not assume that American-style food is any safer than the native food in areas with poor sanitation and hygiene. The general rule in Risk Level II and III areas is: *Cook it, peel it, or forget it.*

Fruits and vegetables may be contaminated with bacteria if they have been grown with human fertilizer. Cooking is the best protection. Avoid all raw fruits and vegetables except those with thick, intact skins you can peel yourself and eat after washing your hands with clean water. Avoid raw salads.

Never eat raw meats, poultry, egg dishes, fish, or shellfish. These dishes should be cooked thoroughly and eaten while still hot.

Milk and dairy products are unsafe unless they have been pasteurized and kept refrigerated. In areas where milk has not been pasteurized, avoid all milk and dairy products, including cheese, sauces made with milk or cream, ice cream, and dairy-containing desserts. To be safe, boil milk and use dairy products only in foods that are to be cooked. Otherwise, use freshly opened, canned milk or powdered milk mixed with purified water.

Avoid cold meat dishes and cold buffets. Custards, gelatins, creamy desserts, and cream-filled pastries that have not been kept refrigerated also pose hazards. On the other hand, dried baked goods such as bread and cake are generally safe.

Dishes and cutlery may be contaminated. Wipe cutlery with a clean napkin before using.

Avoid roadside food stands unless they appear clean and serve well-cooked food. Flies carry disease, so avoid foods on which flies may have landed.

Infants can safely drink breast milk as well as formula made with boiled water.

Water

Risk Level I countries generally have chlorinated water that meets U.S. standards. In other areas assume that the water is unsafe unless you know otherwise. Safe beverages in Risk Level II and III countries include:

- drinks made with boiled water, such as tea or coffee;
- canned or bottled carbonated beverages, as long as the seal on the bottle is intact, and canned fruit juices (avoid non-carbonated beverages, which may be made from contaminated water);
- beer and wine.

Freezing does not disinfect, so ice cubes are no safer than the water they are made from. If you are served ice in a glass, immediately discard the ice and wipe the glass thoroughly with a clean napkin. This applies to alcoholic beverages as well, because the alcohol in a mixed drink will not reliably kill bacteria.

Before drinking from a can or bottle, wipe the outside of the container with a clean cloth. Better yet, carry your own sanitary straws and use them to drink from the original container.

Do not use unsafe water for brushing your teeth, rinsing dentures, or cleaning contact lenses. Carry contact lens solution. When bathing or showering, avoid getting water in your mouth, eyes, and nose.

Water Purification

Boiling is the most reliable method for purifying water. Bring water to a vigorous boil, and allow it to cool to room temperature in a clean, covered container.

At high altitudes, water boils at a lower temperature. Adjust by boiling water one additional minute for each 1,000 feet above sea level. Carry an immersion coil to boil your own water (you may also need an adapter or a current converter). To correct the flat taste of boiled water, you can add a pinch of salt or pour the water back and forth several times from one clean container to another.

When it is not possible to boil water, the next best purification method is chemical disinfection with iodine. If possible, filter cloudy water before you treat it by passing it through a fine-meshed cloth or paper filter. You can also use one of the lightweight charcoal-based filters available in backpacking and camping stores.

If you are using a two-percent tincture of iodine, be sure your iodine supply is fresh, and keep it tightly closed when you are not using it. Add five drops to each quart or liter of clear water, letting the mixture stand for thirty minutes. If the water is cold or cloudy, use ten drops and let it stand one hour. The water should have a faint yellow color.

You can also use iodine tablets. Globaline®, Potable-Aqua®, Coghlan's®, and other brands are available in sporting goods stores and pharmacies. Follow the manufacturer's directions. Double the number of tablets if the water is cloudy. If the water is cold, warm it or increase the contact time. Check the expiration date on iodine tablets, and keep the bottle tightly capped.

Iodine in excess is poisonous. Do not rely on iodine-treated water for most of your drinking needs. Pregnant women and people allergic to iodine should avoid iodine-treated water. If you have thyroid problems, do not use iodine-treated water without the approval of your doctor.

Other means of purification are less effective. Chlorine in tablet or liquid bleach form has been used to purify water, but it is not as reliable as iodine. Portable filters are also available for treating water. They may sometimes be adequate to remove parasites, but they do not reliably protect against all bacteria and viruses. If no safe drinking water is available, hot tap water may be

used as a last resort. Use tap water that is uncomfortably
hot to the touch, allowing it to cool to room temperature
in a clean, covered container. Don't use it any more than
you have to.

Colds and Flu

Visiting a new area may expose you to strains of
viruses to which you are not accustomed, increasing
your risk of catching cold or flu. Protect yourself by
eating a healthy diet, getting plenty of sleep, controlling
stress, and avoiding crowded, enclosed places where
you may be exposed to viruses.

Constipation

The changes in living patterns which accompany travel
can cause constipation. Make sure that you are getting
enough natural fiber in your diet, even though you may be
avoiding fresh fruits and vegetables. Cooked vegetables
and grains and other starchy staples are good sources of
fiber. Also plan to drink adequate liquids and get plenty of
exercise. These measures should be enough to prevent
constipation most of the time.

Air travel unfortunately provides ideal circumstances
for inducing constipation. Passengers who sit for long
periods can become dehydrated, both because airlines
do not routinely serve water and because the cabin air is
very dry. To prevent constipation on your flight, get up
and move around periodically and drink beverages
without caffeine or alcohol.

Diarrhea

Diarrhea is a common complaint among travelers, especially those visiting developing countries. Diarrhea can
have many possible causes, including bacteria, viruses,
certain foods, food poisoning, even the stress of travel.
Often the cause of traveler's diarrhea is simply unfamiliar
bacteria to which the bowel must become accustomed.
The main danger from diarrhea is dehydration.

Careful observation of the food and water precautions discussed above will help prevent many cases of this discomfort. *Do not take drugs to prevent diarrhea without your doctor's approval.* Antidiarrhea medications can have side effects and may encourage the growth of drug-resistant bacteria.

Heat and Cold

Your body needs time, sometimes a week or more, to adjust to hot climates. To prevent heat-related problems, avoid going out or exercising strenuously during the hottest time of the day, and use air-conditioned hotels, restaurants, and transportation if possible. Wear loose clothing of natural fabrics to allow your perspiration to evaporate. Put on a broad-brimmed hat when you go outside in the sun, and remove it when you are indoors or in the shade.

In hot climates, take steps to prevent water loss. Increase your intake of fluids, but avoid alcohol. If you are performing a lot of strenuous activity, you can increase your salt intake. Otherwise, maintaining a normal level of salt consumption in your diet should be sufficient. However, if you are on a salt-restricted diet because of heart or blood pressure problems, you should consult with your doctor about the advisability of increasing your salt intake. Watch for a darkening of urine, which is a sign of dehydration. Drink enough fluids to keep your urine light in color.

Cold weather activities such as skiing and hiking can expose you to the risks of cold temperature, especially when wind and dampness accompany the cold. Problems caused by exposure to cold, including frostbite and hypothermia, can be quite serious. The very old, the very young, and others with chronic diseases are particularly susceptible to injury from the cold.

Whenever you travel or exercise in cold weather, wear layers of warm, loose clothing, and carry extra dry clothing in case your clothes get wet. Wear gloves or mittens and a hat that covers your ears. Do not drink alcohol or coffee, and do not smoke. Instead, eat high energy foods and drink plenty of non-alcoholic fluids, especially where hypothermia is a potential problem.

High Altitude

Not only trekkers, skiers, and mountain climbers, but even ordinary sightseers are at risk for high altitude (or mountain) sickness. Today's travelers can arrive at high altitudes without having adequate time for their bodies to acclimate. Many ski resorts and mountain cities, for example, can be reached directly by jet planes which abruptly deposit travelers a mile or more above sea level. The result can be mountain sickness, which is caused by a reduction in the amount of oxygen reaching the brain and muscles because of the lower atmospheric pressure at high elevations.

To prevent mountain sickness, take enough time—two or three days—for your body to become accustomed to the higher altitude. Don't plan vigorous activities right away. If you will be flying directly to a high-altitude destination, your doctor might prescribe acetazolamide (Diamox®). However, some people should not take this drug, so medical approval is important.

Mountain sickness is more common at elevations above 10,000 feet, though some people begin to show symptoms at elevations as low as 5,000 feet. Symptoms range from mild discomfort—headache, nausea, sleep difficulties, loss of appetite, shortness of breath, and fatigue—to more acute disorders—confusion, reduced urine output, inability to sleep, intense headache, marked breathing difficulties, delirium, loss of memory, and unconsciousness. Extreme cases of mountain sickness can be quite serious and even fatal.

Trekkers and mountain climbers should allow their bodies to adjust at an altitude of 6,000-8,000 feet for a few days before going higher. You may climb higher during the day, but return to sleep at an elevation no more than 1,000 feet higher than the night before.

In addition to the risk of mountain sickness, high altitude can expose you to intense sun, cold and wind, and dry air. Be sure to protect against all these hazards.

Insect Protection

In many parts of the world insect bites can transmit serious diseases. Mosquito bites cause malaria, yellow fever, dengue fever, filariasis, and Japanese encephalitis. Ticks transmit many diseases, including typhus and Lyme disease. River blindness is carried by blackflies, and the tsetse fly carries African sleeping sickness. Other insects cause illness or discomfort by injecting venom.

The best way to protect yourself against insect-borne diseases is to avoid contact with the insects. Find out the insect hazards in the areas you will be visiting. If these hazards are seasonal or restricted to certain localities, you can plan your itinerary to avoid exposure.

Select your eating and sleeping accommodations carefully. Choose an air-conditioned or well-screened hotel that is clean and free of insects. Do not eat at outdoor restaurants or buffets, either of which may attract flying insects.

Protect against lice, scabies, and bedbugs by making sure that your bedding is clean and has a freshly-laundered smell. Where insects like spiders and scorpions are common, shake out clothing and footwear before you put them on, and never stick your hand or foot where you cannot see. If you plan to travel off the normal tourist routes, carry a sheet sack. This is a sheet sewn together along the sides to form a sleeping bag which can be used on top of straw mats or mattresses of questionable cleanliness.

Find out the time of day when insects are likely to bite. The mosquitos which carry malaria, for example, usually bite between dusk and dawn. Avoid outdoor exposure at these times, and make sure you are well protected if you go outdoors. Use insect repellent and wear clothing heavy enough to prevent insects from biting through it. Cover your body well with long sleeves and long pants. Don't wear perfumes or scented cosmetics, jewelry, or bright clothing, all of which attract some insects. Pale colors such as khaki, tan, or light green are preferable. Do not go barefoot.

The most effective insect repellent for mosquitoes is deet (n,n-diethyl-meta-toluamide), in a relatively high concentration for adults (60-80%) and lower for children and pregnant women (50-60%). Deet can be applied to both skin and clothes. It is water-soluble, so reapply the repellent after swimming, sweat, or walking in the rain. *Deet can be toxic, especially to children.* Don't use it any more than you have to and be sure to wash it off completely at the end of each day.

Spray pyrethrin insecticide (available in most camping supply stores) around sleeping and other indoor areas. Sleep with netting over your bed. Permethrin, a synthetic form of pyrethrin, can be applied to the clothes. Use it on your garments and deet on your skin for maximum protection.

Sit on a blanket or towel at beaches or pools. Always shake out your clothes and shoes before putting them back on. Stay away from stagnant water and small ponds where mosquitoes are likely to breed.

Ticks and blackflies tend to resist insect repellents more than mosquitoes. Be prepared to examine your entire body carefully anytime you have been outdoors in tick-infested areas. Before you risk exposure, review Sidebar 3A (page 60), which discusses the safe way to remove ticks.

Personal Hygiene

Pay careful attention to personal cleanliness during your travels. Keep your clothes clean and dry, and change them daily. Bathe at least once a day and dry yourself thoroughly, especially in the skin folds, to prevent skin infections. Using powder after bathing may help you keep dry. Do not put your fingers in your mouth, and always wash your hands before eating or preparing food.

Because it is easy to pick up fungus infections and hookworms, do not go barefoot and do not sit on the ground with exposed skin. Avoid swimming or wading in fresh water or in any water that may be contaminated. (See "Swimming and Bathing," page 53).

Safe Sex

Sexually active travelers are at risk for sexually transmitted diseases (STDs), including AIDS and others that are resistant to the usual antibiotics. The only certain ways to avoid catching an STD are abstaining from sexual contact entirely or restricting sexual activity to one partner who you know does not have any STDs.

If you do choose to have sex with a partner or partners whose health status is unknown, the following precautions will reduce your chances of infection. They will not guarantee your safety, however.

- Use condoms along with nonoxynol-9 spermicide to help protect against the transmission of STDs. Diaphragms and contraceptive jellies, creams, and foams offer some protection, but they are less reliable than condoms.
- Women who use diaphragms or birth control pills should use condoms and spermicide in addition.
- Ask your partner whether he or she has any STDs and do not have sex with anyone who does.
- Wash your genitals and those of your partner carefully before any sexual contact.
- Urinate after intercourse.
- Do not have sex with anyone who has genital sores, discharges, or warts.
- Avoid genital contact with cold sores on the mouth.
- Avoid unprotected anal contact.
- Do not rely on antibiotics before sex as a way of preventing STDs.

Additional information about preventing STDs while traveling can be found in the "Sexually Transmitted Diseases" section of Chapter 3 (pages 81-84).

Snakes

Most poisonous snakes are not aggressive, and most snakebites are inflicted by nonpoisonous species. If you plan to stay in a remote area, ask the local residents about the native species of poisonous snakes and their habits. Wear long pants and high boots in snake-infested areas. Never step or reach out blindly. Check your footwear before you put it on. Use a flashlight at night. If possible, sleep on an elevated bed or cot when you are outdoors. If you encounter a snake at close quarters and it appears to be threatening, keep absolutely still.

Sun Protection

You can develop a painful sunburn quickly while traveling, especially in the tropics, at high altitudes, and on the water. If you do not already have a protective tan, you will need to take measures to avoid excessive sun exposure. Wear a hat and light-colored clothing that covers the arms and legs. Use a protective sunscreen cream or lotion with a sun protection factor (SPF) of at least fifteen if you are fair-skinned or do not already have a tan. PABA (para-aminobenzoic acid) provides the best protection, but it can produce rashes in some people. Apply sunscreen before going into the sun, and reapply it after sweating or swimming. Limit your sun exposure to twenty minutes the first day, and gradually increase it as you develop a tan. Remember that you can get sunburned even on overcast days and that the sun's rays can penetrate thin clothing.

Some drugs, such as tetracycline, may produce extreme sensitivity to sunlight. Your doctor can tell you if any of your medications can cause photosensitivity.

Skiers and hikers should be extra careful to protect their skin and eyes, especially at elevation, with a high-

SPF sunscreen and dark goggles. Because the sun's rays are less filtered by the atmosphere at high altitudes, ultraviolet exposure can be much more extreme. This can cause a serious sunburn in a surprisingly short time. Your eyes also require special protection to guard against sun- or snowblindness. Dark gray or green lenses are best for protecting against ultraviolet rays.

Swimming and Bathing

Never swim or wade in fresh-water lakes and streams in tropical areas. They present a risk of infection from schistosomiasis and potentially expose you to mosquitoes and other insects which transmit serious disease. If you are accidentally exposed to fresh water, dry yourself vigorously with a towel and apply rubbing alcohol. Even bath water should be boiled or chlorinated in Risk Level III areas where water-borne parasites are a danger. Chlorinated pools are generally safe if they are well maintained.

Salt-water swimming does not present the same risks of exposure to disease-carrying organisms, but you should avoid the potentially polluted beaches near cities or river mouths. If you do swim in sea water near populated areas, keep your head out of the water to prevent infections. Always be on the alert for poisonous plants or animals, as well as for sharks.

Use a towel or mat on the beach to avoid picking up parasites.

Chapter 3

Treating Common Health Problems

If a health problem does arise during your trip, you may need to administer some care yourself. This chapter will give you information to help you take care of minor problems when medical help is not available and recognize when a problem is serious enough to require medical care. It also offers general advice about what to do while you are waiting for professional help.

However, this chapter is not intended to substitute for medical attention or to replace medical treatment. The symptoms, medications, dosages, and treatments included are not exhaustive. They are generally appropriate for the average person, but individual health conditions may call for special considerations. A good rule of thumb always is: *When in doubt, see a doctor.*

The recommendations of your personal doctor should always take precedence whenever any medical problems arise. Pay particular attention to the warning signs which indicate that a health problem or disease is serious enough to require medical care. (For further information on some of these diseases, see Appendix E.)

Do not attempt to treat diseases or serious health problems yourself, and never self-prescribe medications that can be purchased at pharmacies abroad. It is safest to restrict your use of medications to those which you brought from home in your medical kit, all of which should have been evaluated by your doctor in light of your own medical history.

Always seek professional advice whenever you experience a health problem while traveling. Consult Chapter 4, "Getting Medical Help Abroad," if you are having difficulty finding a doctor. Sometimes, you may have no alternative but to begin treatment yourself for a serious medical problem. The information in this section may help you handle these situations until you can receive the medical attention you need. But you should always seek out immediate professional attention whenever you make a medical judgment.

Abdominal Pain

Travelers may experience abdominal pain for a variety of reasons—unfamiliar foods, the stress of traveling, exertion after eating, or any number of diseases, for example. If it is indigestion, the victim will usually experience a burning pain in the mid-chest, or just over the stomach under the breastbone. Indigestion will normally be relieved by an antacid or milk (make sure it is pasteurized). Try to determine what caused the pain, and avoid it in the future.

Abdominal pain can also be a sign of serious problems, however. In women, it may be caused by pelvic inflammatory disease or ectopic pregnancy.

Severe, steady pain in the right lower quadrant of the abdomen, with vomiting but without diarrhea, may be a sign of appendicitis. This is a medical emergency calling for immediate medical attention.

Never take laxatives if you are having severe abdominal pain.

Abdominal pain can also be a sign of a heart attack. See the discussion of "Chest Pain" below.

Allergic Reactions

For some people, severe allergic reactions can result from bee or wasp stings or from consuming certain foods or medicines. If you know that you have a severe allergy to a medication or to insect stings, you should wear an identifying bracelet. If you are carrying inject-able epinephrine and an antihistamine, make sure you know how to use them.

Signs of a serious allergic reaction, or anaphylaxis, are wheezing, difficulty breathing, tightness in the throat, an undetectable pulse, and possibly a skin rash. *Anaphylaxis is a potentially life-threatening emergency.* Seek medical help immediately. You may also need to give mouth-to-mouth resuscitation or CPR to keep the victim breathing. Both of these first-aid techniques are described below under "Emergencies" (pages 69-73).

Bites and Stings

Animal bites

Bites of dogs, cats, and other mammals can cause a number of health problems, including infections, teta-nus, and rabies. To prevent infection, immediately clean the bite wound thoroughly with soap and clean water, and flush it with copious amounts of water. Do not try to close the wound. Get to a doctor, who will usually give an antibiotic. If you have had a tetanus booster before traveling, you probably will not need to worry about tetanus.

Wild animals as well as urban dogs may carry rabies. Any animal behaving strangely or biting without provo-cation should be suspected of being rabid. If you are bitten by such an animal, seek medical attention imme-diately for rabies treatment. If possible, capture the animal so it can be taken to a laboratory for examination.

In developing countries, the rabies treatments avail-able are not as free of side effects as the new human

diploid cell vaccine (HDCV) used in the United States.
Still, get treatment as soon as possible. Then, as quickly
as you can, find a center where the more advanced
anti-rabies vaccines are available. If the American embassy or consulate does not have its own stock of HDCV,
it will be able to direct you to a source of treatment.

Insect and spider bites

People who are sensitive to bee or wasp stings may
experience severe allergic reactions. Because they can be life
threatening, these reactions must be taken very seriously (see
"Allergic Reactions", page 57). If you are stung and fear you
may have a serious reaction, take an antihistamine such as
diphenhydramine (Benadryl®, for example), which is often
available over the counter. If the stinger is still in the skin,
remove it, but do so carefully to avoid injecting more poison.
To relieve discomfort, apply ice, a paste of meat tenderizer
and water, or a papaya poultice. Watch for symptoms of
complication. Severe allergic reactions usually occur within
the first fifteen minutes after the bite, and almost always
within a few hours.

Spider bites can be quite painful, but they are rarely
life-threatening. They present a greater risk to children
than to adults. Apply ice to a spider bite and immobilize
the area. The spider may cling to the bite, in which case
you will be able to identify it. Some spider bites, such
as those of the black widow, need to be treated by a doctor
with antivenin, so if there is any question about identity,
bring the spider with you.

Scorpions are nocturnal relatives of spiders. Be careful
where you walk or put your hands at night, and shake out
your boots or shoes before you put them on in the morning.
Scorpion stings are rarely dangerous for adults, although
they can be for children. The sting may be painful, but it
will normally get better on its own. Aspirin (for adults) and
ice applications will help to relieve the pain. Persistent
numbness and pain can be relieved with hot compresses.

Sea creatures

Many species of marine creatures are poisonous. Before going into the water, ask local residents whether any poisonous species inhabit the local waters and, if they do, how to identify them and how to treat their stings. For many sea creatures, such as jellyfish and stingrays, the treatment is similar:

- Rinse the wound thoroughly to dilute the toxin.
- Give an appropriate pain medicine if necessary.
- Wrap the injured area in cloth.
- Get medical help.

Snakebites

Poisonous snake do not always inject venom when they bite people. However, pain, numbness, tingling, swelling of the bitten part, or shallow breathing or lightheadedness, all suggest that venom was injected. If you can, identify the snake or kill it so it can be brought in for identification. Be very careful when handling even an apparently dead snake, using a sack and a stick instead of bare hands.

The treatment for poisonous snakebite depends on the species of snake. The general instructions are:

- Keep the victim quiet and calm to minimize the circulation of poison through the body.
- Do not try to cut the wound open or suck out the venom.
- Do not use a tourniquet. Instead, wrap the bitten area immediately with a firmly fitting dressing of bandages or strips of cloth. If the bite is on an arm or leg, wrap the entire limb and immobilize it with a splint.
- Encourage the victim to drink liquids, but not alcohol.
- Get the victim immediately to medical care.

HOW TO REMOVE A TICK

Do not just tear a tick away from your body with your fingers; you may leave body parts of the insect embedded in your skin.

Using tweezers, grab the body of the tick close to the skin and pull straight out with a gentle, steady motion.

Do not squeeze the tick. Do not try to make it let go by applying a burning match, or Vaseline, gasoline, or other chemicals. This may cause the tick to release bacteria into your body.

Save the tick for examination by a doctor if there is any chance it may be carrying a serious disease. Wash the bite with soap and clean water. During the following days, be alert for signs of illness such as fever, headache, or rash.

If you are unable to remove the tick by yourself or if a complication occurs, get immediate medical help.

(Sidebar 3A)

Ticks and leeches

Tick bites by themselves are not usually harmful, but in some areas ticks can transmit serious diseases. After every outing in tick-infested areas, examine your body and look for ticks. If you do find a tick, remove it carefully following the instructions found in Sidebar 3A., above.

Leeches are found both on land in tropical rain forests and in the water. Check whenever you feel any unusual sensation on your skin. Remove a leech by heating it with a cigarette or a match or by applying salt, alcohol, or iodine. The leech will let go by itself in any case once it has finished feeding. Wash the wound with soap and water.

Bleeding

To control bleeding from a wound, raise the injured part above the level of the heart. Apply pressure over the wound with a clean cloth or a hand. It may take fifteen minutes or more for the bleeding to stop. If the cloth becomes saturated with blood, do not remove it. Instead, add more cloth. Do not use a tourniquet, which may cause gangrene. If the bleeding is severe, get immediate medical attention.

Blisters

Blisters are usually caused by badly fitting footwear. Prevent irritation by wearing two pairs of socks, a thin synthetic inner pair and a heavy outer pair. At the first sign of irritation, stop walking and put some moleskin or tape over the area to prevent a blister from forming.

If a blister does form, sterilize a needle by holding it in a flame. Pierce the blister with the sterilized needle, then cover it with a loose sterile dressing for a day or two. An alternative treatment is to leave the blister intact and to cushion it with layers of moleskin from which holes have been cut out.

Broken Bones and Dislocations

Broken bones or dislocations should be treated by a doctor as soon as possible. Examine the injured area to locate the area of maximum tenderness. If a fracture is present, you may feel a separation in the bone or a swelling and tenderness localized to the bone. The normally severe pain of a fracture may prevent movement of the injured part. Immobilize the bone with a temporary splint, then get medical help. You can improvise a splint from rolled-up newspapers, branches, a foam pad, or anything else which will keep the fractured bone immovable.

Burns (including Sunburn)

For minor burns which do not form blisters, immediately apply ice or ice water for twenty minutes to relieve pain and minimize damage. If the burn causes blisters, apply ice or ice water as above, then cover the burn with a dry, sterile dressing. Keep the burned part above the level of the heart to minimize pain. If the blisters are broken, wash them gently with cooled, boiled water, then remove the dead skin. Cover the cleansed blister with a thin, sterile gauze dressing, which should be changed every twelve hours. Keep the burn very clean, making sure it is not exposed it to dirt or flies.

If signs of infection appear—pus, fever, tender or swollen lymph nodes, or a bad smell—apply warm salt water compresses (a teaspoon of salt to a quart water) three times a day. Be sure to boil both the water and the cloth before using. Get medical attention whenever a burn becomes infected.

A burn is serious if it covers a large area (more than the size of the hand) or if the skin is charred. Get medical help immediately. In the meantime, wrap the burned area loosely in very clean cloth, reassure the victim, and give plenty of liquids (preferably Rehydration Drink) as long as the victim is not vomiting.

Sunburn

Sunburn can be treated with cold compresses, while aspirin (for adults) or acetaminophen can be taken to reduce the pain. Severe sunburn with blistered skin should receive medical attention.

Chest Pain

While chest pain can be a symptom of heart disease, it also has many other possible causes, including indigestion, ulcers, muscle strain, and lung infection. Heart-related chest pain may be accompanied by sweating or shortness of breath. It may radiate to the neck or the arm, and it may last from hours to days. If you have a history of heart disease, or if you are over fifty years of age and have risk factors such as heart disease in your family, high blood pressure, cigarette smoking, or diabetes, seek medical help in the event you experience chest pain.

If you are having chest pain that you suspect may be a heart attack, avoid exertion and have yourself transported to a medical center for emergency treatment.

Colds and Flu

Treat cold symptoms early. At the first appearance of a sore throat, a runny nose, or a slight cough, start drinking lots of fluids and get plenty of rest. You may take aspirin or acetaminophen to reduce fever and relieve minor aches and pains. (To minimize the risk of Reye's Syndrome, do not give aspirin to anyone under the age of twenty.) Do not take antibiotics for flu—they are not effective against viruses. If possible, avoid flying when your head is stuffed up. If you must fly, use an antihistamine decongestant, nose drops, or nasal spray to relieve congestion, especially during takeoff and landing.

It is not unusual for children to have a high fever with a cold, but a persistent high fever, and any fever with swollen glands and sore throat, should receive medical attention. Observe infants carefully. If they show a lack of interest in eating, drinking, or their surroundings, get medical help immediately.

Early treatment of a cold or flu will prevent its progression to pneumonia. Anyone who is at risk of pneumonia (elderly people or people with respiratory diseases) and who has not had a flu shot should be careful to watch for signs of worsening condition: rapid, shallow breathing; wheezing; a cough with yellow, greenish, or bloody sputum; or chest pain. If you develop any of these symptoms, seek medical attention immediately. In the meantime, drink plenty of liquids, take aspirin or acetaminophen to reduce fever and pain, and breathe hot water vapors to loosen mucus. Again, people under the age of twenty should not be given aspirin.

Constipation and Hemorrhoids

Constipation is usually a temporary condition, often brought on by changes in life style or environment. The general recommendations for preventing constipation—eating enough fiber, drinking sufficient liquids, getting moderate exercise—will also help to correct it.

Should you find yourself constipated, relax, take a walk, and eat smaller meals until your constipation is over, and don't strain at the toilet. Take a mild laxative if necessary, but not if you have stomach pain. Constipation will normally take care of itself in a few days. Seek medical advice if does not clear up in a reasonable amount of time, if it is accompanied by blood in the stool, or if your belly is swollen at the same time.

Avoiding constipation also helps to prevent hemorrhoids. A high-fiber diet with plenty of fluids will help prevent both. If you should develop hemorrhoids, take warm sitz baths every few hours. Shallowly fill a tub with hot water, and sit in the bath for at least fifteen minutes. Stay off your feet as much as possible until the symptoms subside.

Cuts, Wounds, and Scrapes

Clean all wound very carefully to prevent infection, especially in the tropics and wherever sanitation standards are poor. After washing your hands with soap and water, cleanse the wound thoroughly with mild soap and previously boiled water. Clean all dirt from the wound, using gauze or, if necessary, tweezers that have been sterilized by boiling. Flush out the wound for at least five minutes with large quantities of previously boiled water, preferably with salt added (3/4 teaspoon per quart). Be sure that there is no foreign material left in the wound, and get medical help if any remains.

Once you are sure the wound is thoroughly clean, cover it with a light dressing of clean gauze. Change the dressing every day, more frequently if it becomes soiled. If you have not had a tetanus booster, get one. Do not put alcohol, tincture of iodine, or merthiolate into a wound. These can cause tissue damage and will slow healing.

Monitor the wound carefully for infection. Signs of infection are redness, heat, pain, pus, and a bad smell. If the wound is accompanied by a fever, a red streak running from the wound, or tender or swollen lymph

---

REHYDRATION DRINKS

Oral Rehydration Formula

You can have a pharmacist make up packets of Oral Rehydration Formula for your medical kit. It is also available from IAMAT (see Chapter 1, page. 27). Each packet should contain:

> **20.0 grams glucose**
> **3.5 grams NaCl**
> **2.5 grams NaHCO3**
> **1.5 grams KCl**

Dissolve one packet in one liter of purified water.

(Continued →)

---

nodes between the wound and the center of the body, the infection is spreading. Treat an infected wound with hot compresses for twenty minutes, four times a day. Keep the infected part at rest, elevated above the level of the heart to help relieve pain, and seek medical attention promptly.

Puncture wounds, wounds made with dirty objects, crushing or bruising wounds, bites, bullet wounds, or wounds incurred in places where animals are kept, all present the risk of serious infection. Take special care to keep these wounds clean, watch them closely, and seek medical attention right away.

Dehydration

Dehydration can be caused by diarrhea, vomiting, sweating in hot climates, exertion, or exposure to high altitude. Suspect dehydration if there is little or no urine output and the urine which does come out is dark yellow. Other signs include dizziness, headache, and dry mouth and eyes. To test for dehydration, pinch the skin on the inner forearm for a second, then let it go. The inability of the skin

---

Rehydration Drink

Prepare the following in two clean glasses:

- *Glass #1* Eight (8) oz. (250 ml.) **fruit juice** (preferably orange or apple juice); One-half (1/2) tsp. (2.5 ml) **honey or corn syrup;** Pinch of **salt.**

- *Glass #2* Eight (8) oz. (250 ml) **purified water** or **carbonated bottled water;** One-quarter (1/4) tsp. **baking soda.**

Drink alternately from each glass.
Supplement either Rehydration Drink with other safe beverages, such as purified water, weak tea, or carbonated beverages.
Infants should continue breastfeeding and take Rehydration Drink alternately with sips of pure water.

(Sidebar 3B)

---

to spring back instantly is a sign of dehydration. Give lots of fluids, preferably one of the Rehydration Drinks described in Sidebar 3B. If for any reason you cannot give liquids by mouth, seek medical help immediately.

Dental Problems

Be prepared to deal with small dental emergencies on your own. In many developing countries the preferred treatment is to pull the tooth, no matter what the problem.

Aspirin (adults only) and acetaminophen are effective for reducing most tooth pain. If the pain is in a tooth with a cavity, soak a piece of cotton with oil of cloves and place it in the hole of the cavity to relieve the pain.

If the gum around a tooth is inflamed, remove any debris with dental floss. Then rinse with salt water or bottled hydrogen peroxide solution which you have diluted one part to four with warm, clean water.

A sore tooth with surrounding swelling may indicate the presence of an abscess, especially if fever is present. If there is a cavity, clean it out and insert a cotton pellet soaked with oil of cloves. Take aspirin (adults only) or other pain killers for pain and see a dentist for antibiotic treatment as soon as possible.

If you break a tooth or filling and you are not uncomfortable, you probably do not need immediate treatment. If a broken tooth irritates the tongue or cheek, a temporary covering made from candle wax, chewing gum, or cotton may reduce the irritation.

If a tooth is knocked out with an intact root, you may be able to save it if you can get to a dentist quickly. Soak a tea bag in clean, warm water and place it over the socket, holding it in place with your teeth. Handle the lost tooth by the crown—do not touch the root. Place it in fresh milk or wrap it in wet gauze. As an alternative, you can rinse the tooth in warm water and your mouth with a baking soda solution. Then put the tooth gently back into its socket, holding it in place for at least ten minutes. Get to a dentist immediately.

If your tooth is knocked loose but not out, gently hold it in place it with your fingers, rinse frequently with baking soda solution, take an appropriate analgesic for pain, apply a cold pack for the swelling, and get to a dentist quickly.

If you break a denture, save all the pieces and wear the rest of the denture, if possible. Have the whole denture repaired as quickly as possible.

If you lose a cap and the tooth is sensitive, fill the cap with Vaseline, put the cap on the tooth, and carefully bite it into position. Get dental attention as soon as you can.

Diarrhea

The most important consideration in treating diarrhea is to prevent dehydration. Drink plenty of safe, non-alcoholic liquids, preferably including lots of Rehydration Drink (Sidebar 3B), to replace the fluids and salts lost in the stool. Adults with diarrhea should drink twelve or more cups of liquid a day, while small children should drink four cups a day. Infants with diarrhea should breastfeed, drinking pure water and plenty of Rehydration Drink at the same time. Maintaining hydration alone is usually sufficient to resolve traveler's diarrhea in three to five days, if not sooner. Check your urine output to see if you are maintaining adequate hydration. If your urine is dark yellow in color, you may need more fluids.

Give rehydration a chance to work. If it doesn't, anti-diarrhea medications are available. Over-the-counter remedies, such as Pepto-Bismol®, will usually help settle mild to moderate diarrhea. Take two to four tablets, or two tablespoons of liquid, every thirty minutes, up to eight times a day. **Note:** do not take a bismuth subsalicylate such as Pepto-Bismol® if you are taking a blood thinner (aspirin or a warfarin compound like Coumadin®) or if you are allergic to salicylates, have stomach ulcers, or are pregnant. Discontinue the medication as soon as the diarrhea has cleared up.

For more severe diarrhea without blood or mucus, your doctor may recommend an antibiotic such as double-strength TMP/SMZ (Bactrim® or Septra®, for example), one tablet twice a day for three days, along with loperamide (Imodium®), four mg. initially, followed by two mg. after each loose stool, up to a total of sixteen mg. a day. Two daily doses of Cipro® in 250 mg. doses may be prescribed for use with the Imodium. As with all medications, the prescription of these antidiarrhea drugs should be left to a doctor.

Caution: Be wary of some of the antidiarrheal drugs available over the counter in other countries. Some are potentially dangerous and should be avoided. Stay away from drugs like Enterovioform (Mexiform), which is not sold in the United States because it is capable of causing eye and nerve damage.

Very severe diarrhea with blood or mucus in the stool and sometimes with fever is called dysentery. It can be caused by either bacteria or amoebas and requires medical attention to determine the cause and prescribe treatment. Giardiasis is another infection that can cause diarrhea and also calls for medical attention. Both dysentery and Giardiasis are described in Appendix E.

Ear Problems

An ear ache is not always a sign that something is seriously wrong, but ear pain associated with fever is a symptom of ear infection. Seek medical care for proper antibiotic treatment. If your child has a history of ear infections, your pediatrician may have prescribed a supply of the medication you have used to treat the problem in the past. If you are in a remote area and you are carrying the appropriate antibiotic in your medical kit, use it in the prescribed dosage for ten days or the period your doctor prescribed.

Swimmers may develop a discharge from the ear, possibly with inflammation of the ear canal, itching, or mild pain. For 'swimmer's ear,' apply one or two drops of a weak vinegar solution to a cotton wick and insert it into the ear four times a day. This will help dry out the ear. Boric acid ear drops will also help clear up this problem. Avoid swimming while the problem persists. To prevent swimmer's ear, keep your ears dry and shake out all water after swimming.

If you experience temporary ear pain as a result of changes in pressure when you fly, try using a nasal decongestant spray or drops before takeoff and landing. The same precautions can also be used before diving if you experience ear discomfort from changing water pressure.

If an insect crawls into your ear, pour in a nontoxic liquid such as mineral oil or alcohol, and then flush it out with the bulb syringe in your medical kit.

Emergencies

All of the following emergencies require medical assistance. Some first aid may be necessary to save a life, but do not attempt to be your own doctor. Get medical treatment right away.

HEIMLICH MANEUVER FOR CHOKING

Stand behind the victim and wrap your arms around the waist. With both hands together just below the ribs, make a fist with the bottom hand and give several sudden, forceful upward thrusts to force the air out of the lungs and help clear the throat. Repeat if necessary.

If the victim is lying down or if he or she is much larger than you, place the victim face up with the head tilted to one side. Straddle the victim and put your hands together below the ribs as described above. With the heel of the hand give several sudden, strong upward thrusts, repeating as often as necessary.

If the victim is a child, place the child face down across your knees with the head low, and give four sharp blows between the shoulder blades. If that doesn't work, turn the child over and carefully apply four upward chest thrusts, just below the ribs.

If the victim still cannot breathe, give mouth-to-mouth resuscitation.

(Sidebar 3C)

Choking

If food or some other object becomes lodged in a person's throat and interferes with talking or breathing, consider applying the Heimlich maneuver. Sidebar 3C reviews this technique. Immediately seek medical care.

Mouth-to-Mouth Resuscitation

Remove anything stuck in the mouth and pull the tongue forward to make sure it is not blocking the airway. If mucus is blocking the throat, try to clear the passage.

Place the victim face up with the head tilted back. Pull the jaw forward. Pinch the nostrils shut and open the mouth wide. Cover the victim's mouth with yours and blow into the lungs until the chest rises. Take your mouth away to let the air come out, then blow in again.

CARDIOPULMONARY RESUSCITATION

Cardiopulminary resuscitation includes cardiac compression, which cannot be practiced effectively without formal training. If you have received instruction in CPR from the American Red Cross or another agency, the following may help refresh your memory in the event of a crisis.

Confirm that the victim actually requires CPR and has not simply fainted.

Make sure the air passage is clear, and initiate mouth-to-mouth resuscitation.

If breathing does not resume and no pulse can be detected, begin cardiac compression at the correct point beneath the breastbone. Remember to keep the heels of your hands together.

Compress eighty times per minute, administering two breaths after each fifteen compressions.

If you have assistance, one of you can give sixty compressions a minute while another person gives a breath after every five compressions.

Get medical attention immediately.

(Sidebar 3D)

Blow into the lungs about fifteen times a minute. Continue this procedure until the victim can breathe independently (this may take as long as an hour), until medical help arrives, or until you are sure that the situation is hopeless .

Cardiopulmonary Resuscitation (CPR)

CPR is used to restore breathing and heartbeat in medical emergencies. *It should be performed only by a trained practitioner.* If you have received training in CPR, you can refresh your memory by referring to Sidebar 3D. Immediately notify medical authorities.

Unconsciousness

Unconsciousness can have a number of different causes, including fainting, head injury, seizure, stroke, heart attack, intoxication, poisoning, hypothermia, shock, altitude sickness, and heat stroke, among many others.

Simple fainting may not be a serious problem. A person who has fainted may be moist with sweat. Raise the legs above the level of the head and the fainting victim should recover.

Otherwise, try to determine why the victim is unconscious and get medical treament right away. Make sure the victim can breathe. Check that the airway is clear and remove any obstructions. You may need to give mouth-to-mouth resuscitation.

Get immediate medical help.

Shock

Shock is a condition that is best determined by a health professional. Suspect the possibility whenever there has been a serious injury, a severe allergic reaction, dehydration, or serious illness. The symptoms of shock include weak, rapid pulse; cold, damp, pale skin; confusion; weakness; and possibly unconsciousness. If any of these symptoms appear, lay the victim down with the feet above the head. If the victim is cold, cover with a light blanket. Give copious non-alcoholic fluids to drink if the victim is conscious. Be reassuring and get medical help right away.

Near-Drowning

If you rescue someone who has been drowning, begin mouth-to-mouth resuscitation (see above, pages 70-71) as soon as possible, even before the victim is out of the water. Do not take the time to get the water out of the chest before starting resuscitation.

Once the victim is on shore, if you are not able to blow air into the lungs, lay the victim down face up with the head below the level of the feet, and do the Heimlich maneuver, as described in Sidebar 3C. Then continue mouth-to-mouth resuscitation.

Seek immediate medical attention.

Eye Problems

If you wear contact lenses, carry contact lens cleaning and soaking supplies with you so you will not need to rely on potentially unsafe local water. Be prepared to use glasses if any problems develop.

Sunblindness or snowblindness can result from excessive exposure to sun or glare at high altitudes, on snow, or on water. Protect your eyes from the sun by using good lenses that screen ultraviolet. If you feel pain or grittiness on moving the eyelids, patch the eyes and allow them to rest. Seek medical help if you experience problems with vision or if the pain doesn't clear up in a few days.

Pain or burning in the eye, with blurry or decreased vision, should receive immediate medical attention. Remove contact lenses if you are wearing them, and use glasses instead.

'Pink eye,' or conjunctivitis, is a contagious infection of the eyes characterized by redness and swelling of the eyes with pus and a burning or itching sensation. The eyelids may stick together during sleep. Use a clean cloth moistened with boiled water to remove pus. If the condition persists, see a doctor. To help prevent spreading the infection, wash your hands after touching your eyes and do not share towels with other people.

Conjunctivitis can sometimes also be an allergic reaction to pollens or other substances in the air. If it is simply an allergic reaction, it is not contagious and may be helped by taking an antihistamine. Get medical help if there is no improvement.

A sty is an infection in the eyelid that looks like a red, swollen lump. Treated with moist, warm, salt-water compresses, it will eventually drain. A doctor may prescribe ophthalmic antibiotic ointment or drops to prevent a recurrence of the problem.

To remove a foreign body in the eye, grasp the lashes of eyelid under which the object is lodged. Gently lift the lid and pull it over the other lid. This will allow the

underside lashes to work like a brush as the other lid slides
open. Remove anything you see on the white of the eye
with a bit of cotton. Look in the corner of the lower eyelid
if you cannot find anything. A doctor may prescribe antibiotic eyedrops once the foreign body has been removed.
Do not try to remove anything that is firmly stuck in the
eye. Instead, seek medical help right away.

Eye injuries must receive immediate care. If the injury
is caused by a caustic substance such as an acid or other
chemical, rinse the eye with running water for at least ten
minutes and get medical help quickly. For other eye injuries, wash out all dirt and debris with lukewarm, previously
boiled water. Do not try to remove blood clots. Bandage
or patch the eye, give aspirin (for adults), acetaminophen,
or prescribed codeine for pain, and get medical help to
prevent serious damage to the eye.

Fever

Fever is generally a sign of infection. Use a thermometer to check the temperature regularly, and write
down the readings to determine the fever pattern. Some
thermometers may tell temperature in Celsius. Sidebar
3E on the next page will help you convert between
Celsius and Fahrenheit temperatures. A very high fever
(over 104° F) should receive immediate medical attention, as should any fever that persists for more than
twenty-four hours, except in the case of an obviously
minor problem such as a common cold.

Otherwise, reducing a fever may make the sufferer
more comfortable. To reduce fever:

- Take aspirin or acetaminophen. Again, because
  of the association between aspirin and Reye's
  Syndrome, never give anyone under the age of
  twenty aspirin when they have a suspected flu.
- Remove as many clothes as possible and stay
  uncovered.
- Drink plenty of cool liquids to replace fluids
  lost through sweating.

TEMPERATURE CONVERSION

The formulas to convert between Fahrenheit and Celsius are as follows:

Degrees F. = (9 / 5 degrees C.) + 32
Degrees C. = 5 / 9 (degrees F. - 32)

To calculate a Fahrenheit temperature from a Celsius reading, multiply the Celsius temperature by 9, divide the product by 5, and add 32 to the result.

To convert from Celsius to Fahrenheit, subtract 32 from the Fahrenheit temperature, multiply the result by 5, then divide by 9.

Some sample conversions are:

	Fahrenheit	Celsius
Normal temperature	98.6	37
High fever	104	40

(Sidebar 3E)

- Sponge with lukewarm water.

Colds, flu, and infected wounds can cause fever, as can many serious diseases. Suspect malaria in tropical areas where the disease is present if the fever is accompanied by headache and chills. Administer aspirin (not to children) or acetaminophen to bring the fever down, drink plenty of fluids, and get medical attention if you do suspect malaria. Other serious diseases can produce fever, as well. Among these are typhoid, typhus, yellow fever, dengue fever, Japanese encephalitis, meningococcal meningitis, plague, and filariasis, all of which are described in Appendix E.

If an unexplained fever occurs after you have returned home, see your doctor. It could be an infection with a long incubation period.

Heat and Cold

Heat

Heat cramps are a concern whenever traveling in hot climates. Leg, arm, and stomach cramps, sometimes accompanied by vomiting, may occur when people sweat profusely, because perspiration in a hot climate often causes the loss of salt from the body. Prevent heat cramps by getting adequate salt in the diet and drinking plenty of fluids. To treat heat cramps, drink a quart of water with a teaspoon of salt in it every hour until the cramps go away. Rest in a cool place and massage or stretch the sore body part.

Heat exhaustion is a more serious problem, also caused by excessive sweating in hot weather. In heat exhaustion, the body's cooling system is overloaded and needs help to continue working correctly. Signs of heat exhaustion are: a rapid pulse; a temperature ranging from normal to 102° Fahrenheit; cool, moist skin; faintness; and perhaps vomiting or headache. Treat heat exhaustion by resting in the shade, removing excess clothing, and drinking three to five quarts of salt water (1 teaspoon of salt in 1 quart of water) over a twelve-hour period. Recovery is generally rapid. Avoid strenuous activity, and take extra salt for a few days. Consult a physician as soon as possible.

Heat stroke, which is a breakdown of the body's ability to regulate its temperature, is a very serious problem. It especially affects older people, diabetics, alcoholics, and people with poor circulation.

It is important to know the difference between heat stroke and heat exhaustion. In heat stroke the skin will be hot and dry with no sweating. The temperature will be very high—105° Fahrenheit or even more. The pulse will be rapid, and the victim may be unconscious.

Heat stroke is a medical emergency. Take immediate steps to lower the body temperature. Remove excess clothing and immerse the victim in a tub of cool water or soak the victim with wet cloths and supplement by fanning. Continue this treatment until the temperature has dropped below 102° F, then cover the victim with dry clothes or a blanket to prevent chilling. Start giving fluids when the victim is able to take them. Get medical help as soon as possible. The victim should avoid strenuous activity for a few days.

Cold

Frostbite is a freezing of body tissues, usually on the hands, feet, face, or ears. It can cause damage serious enough to require amputation of the injured part if it is not properly treated. At first the affected part feels cold, numb, or painful. Then all feeling disappears as the part freezes. The skin turns pale in color and hardens as it becomes badly frozen. Because there is no feeling in the frozen area, the victim may neglect the problem. Keep an eye on your companions, and let them know if you notice their face or ears turning white or gray.

If the frostbite is mild, treat it by rewarming the affected part. Place it next to warm skin (such as the skin in the armpits or between the thighs) or blow on it with warm breath.

If the tissue is numb, lifeless, and white in color, the frostbite is probably severe. Severe frostbite should not be treated until you are in a dry, warm place where the victim will not need to use the body part.

Until you are able to treat the frostbite, protect against further freezing by keeping the frozen part warm and dry and removing any constricting clothing or jewelry. Do not rub the frozen part with hands, snow, or cloth.

Once you have reached shelter, rewarm the frozen part by immersing it in a large container of warm (not hot) water that is comfortable to the touch (102-108° F or 38-42° C). As the skin warms, it will become painful. Aspirin (not for children), acetaminophen, or codeine (if your doctor has prescribed it) may alleviate some of the pain. Skin color will return to normal as thawing occurs. Keep the victim warm and cover the rewarmed part to prevent further damage. Do not let the victim smoke. Get medical help as soon as possible.

Hypothermia is a reduction of body temperature below normal. It is most likely to develop in cold, wet, windy places. Hypothermia is very dangerous, especially because the victim may be confused and not realize the seriousness of the problem.

The first signs of hypothermia are shivering and a cold feeling. These are followed by dizziness, lack of coordination, confusion, and lethargy. The victim will have difficulty walking and may be hard to get along with. If one of your companions shows any of these signs, suspect hypothermia and treat it immediately. Don't depend on the victim to recognize the symptoms. As the body's temperature drops further, the victim may become indifferent to the cold and fail to take measures to keep warm. Eventually the shivering will stop and the victim may lose consciousness.

To treat mild hypothermia, get to a dry, protected place and make sure the victim is dressed in dry, warm clothes with the head, feet, and hands covered to prevent further heat loss. Give warm, sugary liquids to drink. Rewarm the victim gradually in a sleeping bag or under dry blankets. Have one or more other people get in and hug the victim to keep him or her warm. Do not give alcohol. Encourage the victim to move the arms and legs, which will help rewarm the body.

In severe hypothermia, the victim will not be shivering and may be unconscious. *This is a serious medical emergency.* Move the victim very gently to a protected place. Rewarm the victim gradually by removing the victim's clothes, putting the victim in the warmest sleeping bag available, and piling other warm things on top. You can use hot water bottles or rocks warmed in a fire and wrapped in cloth. If the victim is unconscious, do not try to give food or drink. Get medical help quickly even if warming does restore consciousness.

Mountain Sickness

Mountain sickness normally occurs at altitudes above 5,000 feet. It is caused when the thinner air and reduced air pressure at higher elevations diminish the amount of oxygen reaching the brain of the victim.

Mild mountain sickness may include headache, nausea, sleep difficulties, loss of appetite, shortness of breath, and fatigue. Give your body two or three days to adjust to the higher altitude. Do not go any higher during this time and avoid heavy exercise. Engage in light activity instead of spending the day napping.

Serious mountain sickness is marked by severe headache, weakness, shortness of breath even at rest, confusion, reduced urine output, and inability to sleep. If you are hiking with a group, keep an eye on the behavior of your companions, and have anyone who seems to be having problems descend 1,000 to 2,000 feet or more. The symptoms will usually clear up immediately upon descent.

With very serious mountain sickness there may be severe coughing, pronounced difficulty breathing, intense headache and vomiting, extreme sluggishness, delirium, confusion, staggering and lack of coordination, memory loss, and unconsciousness. The brain and lungs are involved, and at this point the victim must descend without delay, accompanied by a strong, healthy person and carried if possible. Give oxygen if it is available and descend at least 2,000 or 3,000 feet.

Nosebleed

Pinch the nostrils shut for ten to fifteen minutes until the bleeding has stopped. Lean forward with the head between the knees. Do not tilt the head back. Once the bleeding stops, rest the nose for twenty-four hours by not blowing it, breathing through it, or sneezing.

If the bleeding won't stop, pack the nostril with clean cotton, preferably moistened with hydrogen peroxide or vaseline. (Leave a bit of cotton sticking out to make removal easier.) Pinch the nose firmly shut with the packing in place, leaving the packing in place for a few hours. Remove the packing carefully after the bleeding has stopped.

If you have a tendency to suffer from nosebleeds, apply some Vaseline inside your nostrils twice a day.

Poisoning and Food Poisoning

You can avoid most cases of food poisoning if you follow the rules for foods discussed in Chapter 2. Mild food poisoning, marked by vomiting, diarrhea, and abdominal cramps, will usually clear up in twenty-four hours. Drink plenty of fluids to maintain hydration.

Some fish and shellfish toxins can cause serious illness. The symptoms can last for a week or more. Besides vomiting, diarrhea, and cramps, fish poisoning may produce numbness, reduced sensitivity to temperature change, loss of coordination, aching joints, and occasionally paralysis. If symptoms come on within thirty minutes of eating tuna or other dark-meat fish, try to induce vomiting if you haven't already vomited. The symptoms of Ciguatera poisoning—numbness and tingling, nausea, vomiting, cramps, watery diarrhea, etc.—may appear two to six hours after eating reef fish. Try to vomit, and maintain hydration with lots of fluids. Get medical attention whenever the fish poisoning is severe.

Common non-food poisons include medicines in overdose, detergent, bleach, rat poison, insecticides, tincture of iodine, gasoline, kerosene, lye, poisonous plants, and rubbing or wood alcohol. Seek medical help for serious cases of poisoning.

Do not induce vomiting if the poisoning was caused by a hydrocarbon like kerosene or gasoline or by a corrosive substance such as acid or lye. If the victim is conscious, have the victim drink milk (if it is safe) or else water or milk of magnesia.

For other poisons, do induce vomiting. Put a finger down the throat or give the victim a tablespoon of syrup of ipecac or a glass of drinking water with soap or salt added. After the stomach has been emptied, give generous amounts of fluid to drink, preferably milk (pasteurized or boiled), flour mixed with water, or beaten eggs to help absorb the poison.

Sexually Transmitted Diseases

Sexually active travelers must be alert to prevent sexually transmitted diseases (STDs). Following the guidelines for safer sex in Chapter 2 will minimize the risk, but they will not guarantee absolute protection from STDs.

The warning signs of STDs are varied. Among women, a vaginal discharge that does not respond to the simple treatments described under Women's Health Concerns below (pages 88-90) may be a sign of an STD and should be treated by a doctor. Any sore on the genitals or swelling of the lymph nodes in the groin or, among men, any discharge from the penis or discomfort upon urination should receive medical attention.

Do not take antibiotics prior to sexual contact as a way of preventing STDs. Many strains of disease are now resistant to the usual antibiotics.

In many parts of the world, seeking help for an STD can be frustrating and embarrassing. Use your list of English-speaking doctors or other sources of local referrals for sympathetic and competent medical care.

If a doctor tells you that you have an STD, inform your sexual partners immediately so they can also get treatment. It is especially important to inform female partners, because women often show no symptoms and may not know they are infected. Be sure to take the prescribed medication for the full amount of time recommended. Do not engage in sexual activity while you are being treated.

Some of the common STDs are the following.

Gonorrhea or 'Clap'

In men, the first symptoms of gonorrhea are a discharge from the penis and difficulty or pain on urination. Symptoms in men appear two to five days after infection. Women may show no symptoms at all, or symptoms such as a slight pain on urination or a vaginal discharge may not appear for weeks. If you or your sexual partner has any of these symptoms, get medical help immediately. Many strains of gonorrhea have become resistant to the usual antibiotics, especially in Asia and Africa, so it is very important to have a doctor determine the correct medication. People may often have a Chlamydia infection (see below) at the same time as they have gonorrhea. Treatment for both may be required.

Chlamydia

Chlamydia is another sexually transmitted disease that affects both men and women. The symptoms are like those of gonorrhea, but less severe. Untreated chlamydia is a major cause of pelvic inflammatory disease (see below) in women. Those being treated for gonorrhea may need to be treated for chlamydia at the same time. Antibiotics are used to treat both diseases.

Syphilis

Potentially a very serious disease, syphilis is on the increase in many parts of the world. The first sign of the disease is a chancre, or sore, that may look like a pimple, blister, or open sore on the genitals, mouth, or other parts of the body. This chancre is painless and may go unnoticed in women if it is inside the vagina. Contact with the chancre will transmit the disease to others. The chancre goes away by itself, but the untreated disease continues to spread. Because syphilis can be life-threatening, early medical treatment is essential.

Herpes

Herpes is a sexually transmitted disease caused by a virus. From two to twenty days after the initial infection, small blisters appear on the lips or genitals. These blisters burst, forming sores which last up to two weeks and then dry up into scabs. During the period when these sores are present, the disease is most easily transmitted, so avoid all sexual contact with anyone who has sores or scabs on the mouth or genitals. There is no definitive cure for herpes.

Pelvic Inflammatory Disease (PID)

PID in women is a severe infection of the reproductive organs, usually caused by gonorrhea or chlamydia. Women who use IUDs are more susceptible to PID. Pelvic or lower back pain and tenderness, especially on movement or sexual intercourse, may be a sign of PID. PID can lead to serious complications, so seek medical treatment promptly.

Acquired Immune Deficiency Syndrome (AIDS)

AIDS is caused by the human immunodeficiency virus (HIV), which is transmitted through the exchange of blood and other bodily fluids. There is no cure for this worldwide disease at present. For those who develop symptoms, it has thus far been fatal. Symptoms may appear a few months to several years after infection with the virus. Because AIDS weakens the immune system, many normally harmless infections can be life-threatening for the AIDS patient.

Patterns of AIDS transmission vary in different parts of the world. In Africa and Southeast Asia, for example, AIDS is largely spread through heterosexual contact, whereas in the United States and Europe to date it has primarily afflicted homosexuals, intravenous drug users who share needles, and recipients of transfusions of contaminated blood. Both heterosexual and homosexual partners of those infected with the virus are at risk. Casual sex between travelers can be especially risky, because unknown sexual partners may have been exposed to a worldwide pool of infection.

To maximize your protection against AIDS, scrupulously observe the rules for safe sex on pages 51-52. In addition to using a condom, use a contraceptive or lubricant containing the spermicide, nonoxynol-9. Do not allow your partner's semen, blood, urine, feces, or vaginal secretions to enter your body. Except in dire emergency, do not accept blood transfusion or other blood products abroad, especially in countries which do not screen blood for the HIV virus. Do not accept any injection, acupuncture treatment, or tattooing unless you are absolutely sure the needle is sterile. Do not share hypodermic needles, toothbrushes, or razors, and carry your own needles if you expect to travel in an area where you might need to receive an injection under otherwise unsanitary conditions.

AIDS is not currently thought to be transmitted by means of casual contact such as hugging, shaking hands, or sharing meals, or through coughing, sneezing, or using swimming pools or toilet seats.

Skin Problems

Boils

Boils are bacterial infections that form painful, hot, red, swollen lumps containing pus near the surface of the skin. Hot, moist compresses made from a towel or washcloth soaked in hot water should be applied to a boil for fifteen minutes at a time, several times a day. Eventually the boil will come to a head and break open by itself. You can carefully puncture the center with a needle or knife sterilized by holding under a flame. Do not squeeze a boil—you will risk spreading the infection. After the boil drains, apply a clean dressing and wash your hands carefully.

Fungus Infections

Heat and humidity promote the growth of fungus. Fungus infections are latent problems everywhere, but they are particularly troublesome in tropical areas. Among the common fungus infections are:

- Athlete's foot, which causes pale, scaly patches and painful, raw areas between the toes and fingers;
- Jock itch, which causes itching in the groin and raw red areas on the inner thighs;
- Ringworm, a raised, reddish eruption on the body, sometimes in a ring shape.

Treat fungus infections by washing the affected part with soap (preferably disinfectant soap) and water, drying it well, and applying an antifungal powder or cream such as miconazole two or three times a day for two to three weeks. Discontinue the antifungal medication if any irritation occurs. Expose the area to sunlight and air if possible, and keep it dry. Perspiration and tight clothing make fungus infections worse. Avoid spreading the infection from one part of the body to another on contaminated towels and clothing by washing these items in hot water.

Jaundice

Jaundice is an abnormal yellowing of the skin and the whites of the eyes, often accompanied by dark colored urine. Hepatitis is a likely cause, though other possible causes include some drugs as well as malaria and other, more serious medical conditions. If jaundice occurs, immediately discontinue all drugs, including antimalaria drugs, and get medical help.

Lice, Scabies, and Other Insect Bites

Some skin irritations are caused from infestation by insects such as lice or scabies. The scabies mite burrows into cracks and folds in the skin. It is transferred from person to person through touch, including sexual contact, and through infested sheets or bedding. The bumpy scabies rash may appear anywhere on the body, especially between the fingers, on the wrists, around the waist, and on the genitals. It is very itchy, especially at night. The burrows look like dirty ridges or streaks. Avoid scratching, which can cause infection. For most cases of scabies, a physician may prescribe that a lindane cream or lotion, such as Kwell®, be applied for twelve hours and then be washed off. Wash all clothes, bedding, and towels in hot water.

Note: Lindane can be toxic for infants. Your doctor can prescribe an alternative medication or provide specific instructions if lindane must be used.

Lice and lice eggs infest the hair shafts of the head, armpits, and pubic area. Apply lindane to the body after a soap-and-water bath. After twelve hours, wash it off. Shampoo thoroughly, then comb lice eggs out of the hair with a fine-toothed comb. Again, do not use lindane on infants. Avoid close contact with anyone who has been infested with lice until they have been successfully treated. Wash all clothes and bedding in hot water for thirty minutes.

Fleas and bedbugs can also produce red, itchy rashes. The itching can be relieved with calamine lotion or, for severe cases, diphenhydramine (such as Benadryl®). Use a sleeping sack and follow the other recommendations in the "Insect Protection" section of Chapter 2 (pages 49-50) if you suspect your bedding is infested with these troublesome pests.

Rashes

Many rashes are caused by allergic reactions to plants such as poison ivy or poison oak and to environmental substances such as soaps, detergents, cosmetics, or jewelry. Try to determine what the irritating material is and avoid contact with it. If the rash is from contact with a plant, wash the area well with soap and water. To relieve itching, use cool water, a baking soda and water solution, or calamine lotion. An antihistamine such as dimenhydrinate (Dramamine®) also helps to relieve itching. However, antihistamines may cause drowsiness, so do not drive while using them. Contact a doctor for any severe rash.

Drug reactions can also produce rashes. If you suspect that a rash may be caused by a drug, discontinue taking the medication. A rash accompanied by fever may be a sign of serious illness. See a doctor to determine the cause.

Sore Throat

Minor sore throats caused by viruses generally go away on their own. Take simple pain medication or use lozenges to relieve irritation. Sore throats may be caused by a number of diseases, however. Consult a doctor whenever a sore throat becomes severe or fails to go away in two or three days.

If a high fever accompanies a sore throat which lasts for three or more days, or if there are white spots in the throat or swollen lymph nodes, the problem may be strep throat. Get to a doctor for a throat culture and treatment with antibiotics if needed.

Diphtheria is another disease that may produce sore throat among those who have not received diphtheria immunizations. Diptheria calls for medical attention.

Sprains and Strains

A sprain is a tear in a ligament holding bones together at a joint, usually the knee or ankle. Swelling occurs over the area of injury. Carefully feel the injured area to find the point of maximum tenderness. If it is not right over a bone and if you can walk without great discomfort, it may be a sprain rather than a broken bone.

Gently wrap the sprained joint with an elastic bandage, such as an Ace® bandage, to provide firm support to the joint. Apply ice or cold, wet cloths during the first twenty-four hours, keeping the sprain elevated above the heart. Give pain medication if necessary. Stay off the injured part. After twenty-four hours, soak the sprained joint in warm water several times a day. A serious sprain can take up to three or four weeks to heal. If in doubt, seek medical care.

A strain is a pulled muscle, usually from overexertion. Treat it the same as a sprain, applying ice for the first twenty-four hours after the injury and resting the injured area.

Vomiting

Nausea and vomiting may be caused by motion, high altitude, infections, poisoning, or illnesses such as influenza and hepatitis. The most important part of treatment is to avoid dehydration. Give frequent small sips of Rehydration Drink (see Sidebar 3B, pages 65-66), weak tea, or carbonated beverages. Medications for nausea and vomiting include promethazine (Phenergan®) tablets or rectal suppositories and dimenhydrinate (Dramamine®) tablets; or scopolamine (Transderm Scop®) disks. You may already be carrying these medications in your medical kit for the control of motion sickness.

Seek immediate medical help if vomiting is accompanied by such danger signs as:

- Severe vomiting for more than twenty-four hours;
- Vomiting of dark green, brown, or fecal smelling material;
- Blood in the vomit;
- Constant pain in the abdomen;
- Increasing dehydration.

Women's Health Concerns

Menstruation

You can buy sanitary napkins in all but the most remote areas. Tampons are harder to find, so bring supplies from home.

It is not unusual to experience irregular or missed menstrual periods while traveling abroad. If there is any chance of pregnancy, however, have appropriate testing done. If you discover you are pregnant, it is probably wise to return home for care, especially if you are traveling in undeveloped areas.

Painful Urination (Bladder Infection; Cystitis)

Frequent burning or painful urination of small amounts, accompanied by a feeling that the bladder does not empty, may be a symptom of a bladder infection. The urine may contain blood or pus, and it may look cloudy or have a bad smell.

Bladder infections are generally caused by bacteria in the urinary tract, often as a result of sexual activity.

Prolonged sitting and infrequent bathing can also contribute to the problem. To prevent bladder infections, drink plenty of fluids regularly; wipe from the front to the back after using the toilet; and always urinate after sexual intercourse. Avoid tight pants or synthetic underwear.

Drinking large quantities of fluids—at least one glass every thirty minutes—may be sufficient to cure a mild infection. Including large amounts of unsweetened cranberry, orange, or grapefruit juice will make the urine more acidic and inhibit the growth of bacteria.

If the problem does not go away after drinking liquids, you will need to see a doctor for medication. Continue to drink ample fluids while you are on the medication. Get adequate sleep. Avoid alcohol and caffeine, both of which irritate the bladder.

If you continue to have symptoms after treatment, or if you have fever or back pain, you may have a kidney infection. Seek medical help to determine the cause of the problem.

Vaginal Discharge

A thick white discharge like yogurt or cottage cheese, accompanied by itching, may indicate a yeast infection, especially if you have recently been on antibiotics. The problem can be aggravated by wearing nylon panties or panty hose, particularly in hot, humid climates. Wearing cotton panties to allow proper airing may prevent the problem from developing in the first place and cure it if it does set in.

At first appearance of the discharge, use a vinegar-and-water douche. If the infection doesn't go away, get medical treatment. If you have a history of yeast infections, your doctor may have prescribed medication for you to carry on your trip. The usual treatment is nystatin, miconazole, or clotrimazole vaginal suppositories. (**CAUTION:** Because absorbed miconazole may damage a fetus. it should not be used during the first three months of pregnancy.)

Other kinds of vaginal discharges may be clear, thin, frothy, or fishy or foul smelling. Many of these discharges are signs of sexually transmitted infections and should be investigated by a doctor.

If a vaginal discharge is accompanied by pelvic pain and fever, the problem may be pelvic inflammatory disease (see the discussion under STDs, above). Pelvic pain can also be a sign of tubal pregnancy, which requires surgical treatment. Seek medical help immediately for any severe pelvic pain.

Chapter 4

Getting Medical Help Abroad

If you should have a serious health problem while you are traveling, you will need to get competent medical assistance as quickly as possible. As soon as you arrive at any new destination, find out where a good medical facility is located.

Unless you speak the local language, you may want to find an English-speaking physician with whom you can communicate easily. You should already have with you a list of English-speaking doctors for each of your destinations on your *Country Information Worksheet*, or you may be carrying the complete IAMAT *Directory*. Otherwise, carry a phrase book and refer to Appendix D, which is a brief list of some useful emergency and health phrases in five widely-spoken foreign languages.

Sources of Referrals

You should be able to locate reliable medical help in most large, modern cities. If you do not have the name of a local English-speaking doctor, the following sources may result in a referral:

- The U.S. foreign service or the Canadian Representative (see Appendix B) can provide you with

names of local physicians, although they cannot make specific recommendations.

- A local hospital affiliated with a university—preferably a university with a medical school—
  should have a high standard of care and may have
  English-speaking doctors on staff.
- Hospitals run by missionary organizations (such
  as Seventh-Day Adventists) are usually staffed by
  doctors trained in Western medicine.
- If you have travel insurance, an operator on
  your carrier's hotline number may be able to
  provide referrals.
- Volunteer organizations, such as the Peace
  Corps, may be able to refer you to local doctors
  who take care of their volunteers.
- If the telephone book is in English, the listings
  under *Physicians* may include the names of En-
  lish-speaking doctors.
- Managers of large tourist hotels may be able to
  refer you to local doctors. There may even be a
  doctor on the hotel staff.
- Airlines, travel services such as American Ex-
  press, tourist information centers, or local offices of international corporations, all may have
  lists of local doctors.
- American, Canadian, or other English-speaking residents in the area may be able to provide referrals.

Finding medical care may be much more difficult if
you are traveling in remote areas distant from the normal tourist routes. If you plan to spend time in areas far
from medical facilities, be prepared to deal with medical
emergencies. You will need to carry a more complete
medical kit than if you were staying on a normal tourist
route. You should also have an evacuation plan in mind
in case you need to get help in an emergency.

If you do become sick in a remote area, you may be able
to find medical help through medical mission hospitals,
Peace Corps or other volunteer organizations, or American
or other English-speaking residents in the area.

In rural areas, you may be dismayed by the seemingly primitive care and rudimentary facilities offered by the local hospitals. You may need to accept initial treatment wherever you can get it, but you or someone acting as your advocate should keep a close watch on your treatment and be prepared to make decisions about it. If the local care is not adequate for your needs, it is up to you to arrange for more sophisticated treatment. You may need to arrange to be transported to a medical facility in a larger town.

Documenting Your Care Abroad

Be as informed as possible about any treatment you receive from foreign medical personnel, whether it is in a rural clinic or a major urban medical center. Keep careful records of all diagnoses and medical treatments, even if the doctor appears reluctant to provide the information. Ask for copies of examinations such as X-rays, EKGs, or lab tests and for a summary of what was done. Get the names of any drugs you are given, including their generic names, and keep the original labels if possible. You will need to report these drugs to your personal doctor when you return home.

If you have any doubts about the treatment you are receiving, do not hesitate to contact your doctor at home. If possible, have your doctor speak directly to the doctor treating you abroad. Your family doctor knows your medical history, your allergies to drugs, and any other health problems that should be taken into consideration during your treatment.

Many of the medications available in foreign countries are not the same as the drugs that are sold in the United States. Some drugs sold abroad, such as some of the compounds made from chloramphenicol or aminopyrine, may be different enough to be potentially dangerous. Avoid treatment with any drug that you question.

If a transfusion or injection is necessary to save your life, you may have to choose between accepting the risks of the treatment and allowing a life-threatening condition to go untreated. Otherwise, do not permit surgery, injections, or transfusions unless they are absolutely necessary. Blood supplies in many countries may be contaminated with disease-causing organisms, including the lethal AIDS virus. Do not receive any blood transfusion or blood product unless you are certain that it comes from a supply that has been screened for AIDS. Do not accept an injection unless you know the syringe and needle are sterile. Ask to have them sterilized for twenty minutes if you do not see them being removed from a sealed, sterile pack. If you have been traveling in remote, Risk Level III areas, you may be carrying your own sterile needle and syringe in your medical kit. If so, you can ask the doctor to use your needle and syringe.

Get an itemized bill for any medical services you receive. Your insurance carrier may require documentation before it will reimburse you for foreign medical expenses. If you have packed some traveler's insurance claim forms, have them filled out at the time you receive treatment.

Unless your travel insurance plan covers overseas medical treatment, you will probably need to pay at the time you are treated. As part of your travel preparations, you should have arranged for a contact person back home to transfer funds in case of an emergency. U.S. Embassies and consular offices can help arrange for money transfers from home, but they cannot provide emergency funds for medical treatment.

Evacuation

If your life or your future health are in danger because you cannot obtain adequate medical care abroad, you will need to return home or get to a major city where you can obtain proper treatment in a Western-style medical center. If you are in a rural area, you should have made a plan for getting out in an emergency. Finding a phone from which you can call for help may be difficult. Ask the local people to help you find transportation, and have someone you know accompany you during the evacuation. Air ambulance services may be available to transport you to an international airport. You may find the high cost of this service preferable to the slow discomfort of overland travel.

Once you are in a city, contact your travel insurance carrier or the U.S. Embassy or consulate. Both can help arrange your trip back to the United States or to a major city abroad. Evacuation to the United States is usually done by commercial airline. It is very expensive, because the airline will need to block out a number of seats for you on the plane. You will have to pay for these seats in advance. If evacuation costs are not included in your travel insurance coverage, ask your contact person back home to help you get the necessary funds. The U.S. Government will not provide funds for medical evacuation. If you are having difficulty with evacuation arrangements, your contact person can ask for help from the U.S. State Department's Overseas Citizens Emergency Center, 2201 C St., NW, Washington, D.C. (202- 647-5225).

If Someone Dies Abroad

It is a sad responsibility to return the remains of a deceased person to the United States. You will first need to have the death documented by a local official. The death certificate must be translated into English, identifying the body and the cause of death. Traveler's insurance companies and evacuation services may be able to help arrange transportation of the body to an airport. Someone may need to accompany the body, and this will require an additional airfare.

There are no restrictions on bringing a body into the United States, unless the cause of death was cholera, diphtheria, infectious tuberculosis, plague, yellow fever, suspected smallpox, or suspected viral hemorrhagic fevers. If one of these diseases was the cause of death, the body must be cremated or properly embalmed and placed in a hermetically sealed casket. The remains must be accompanied by a properly executed death certificate.

The U.S. Embassy or consulate can arrange to notify the deceased's next of kin at home and assist with the transfer of funds, either to return the body to the United States or to have it buried abroad. The U.S. Government will not cover these expenses, but many traveler's insurance companies do provide for these services.

Chapter 5

After You Return

Some of the diseases which can be acquired abroad may not produce symptoms for several months. It is a good idea to stay alert during the first few months after your return home. If you have any symptoms—especially diarrhea, skin rash, fever, or cough—see a doctor at once.

If you became ill abroad, see a doctor as soon as you get home. Bring with you all the information you have about your diagnosis and treatment, including the names of any medications you were given and their labels, if you have saved them.

Your doctor will need to know your travel history, including the dates of your departure and return, the immunizations you received, the countries you visited and when you visited them, and the antimalaria drugs you took, if any. If you did not plan your trip with your doctor's advice—and even if you did—have all this information with you when you visit the doctor's office.

Your family doctor may or may not be familiar with the kinds of diseases to which you may have been exposed during your travels. Your doctor may refer you to the local health department or to a travel health clinic.

At certain times, you should have a medical check-up following your return even if you remained healthy during your trip. If you spent a prolonged period in an areas of poor sanitation, if you had close contact with the inhabitants of remote areas, if you worked with livestock, or if you had extensive exposure to fresh water or soil in Risk Level III areas, it is a good idea to have a physical examination. This check-up should include a stool examination for intestinal parasites, a repeat tuberculin skin test if your predeparture test was negative, and possibly a blood test and a chest X-ray. Your doctor will recommend the best time to schedule this follow-up medical examination.

If you are returning from a malarious area, be sure to continue taking your antimalaria medication for the full time recommended. If you do come down with a fever, see a doctor immediately and report that you may have been exposed to malaria. Some forms of malaria continue in the liver and may not be eliminated by the usual antimalaria drugs. If there is a chance you were exposed to these forms of malaria, you may require medication with Primaquine after completing the usual antimalaria regimen. Primaquine must be taken under a doctor's supervision, because it can produce serious side effects in people deficient in the enzyme G6PD. Your doctor will order a test for G6PD before prescribing this drug. Note also that if you have traveled in a malarious area and have taken antimalaria drugs, you will not be able to donate blood for the next three years.

The more time passes following your return, the less likely you are to experience any delayed illnesses. After a few months, you can be fairly confident that you probably haven't brought anything back with you. Nevertheless, save your travel records. If you do become ill at any time in the future, the doctor treating you may find useful information in your travel history. Some diseases take years to produce symptoms. Informing your doctor about your past travels may save time, expense, and suffering if a health problem should arise.

Travel health may be a relatively new medical specialty, but its rapid growth has been spurred by our mushrooming knowledge and experience. We all hope that we never need to call upon its expertise. As increasing numbers of people take to the roads, the air, and the sea lanes, it is reassuring to know that individual travelers can do much by themselves to ensure safe and healthy trips. It is equally reassuring to know that capable, competent, and well-informed help is available if we need it.

Bon Voyage!

Appendix A

FORMS AND WORKSHEETS

The forms and worksheets which follow will help you while you are planning and packing for your trip. *The Trip Planning Worksheet* is a checklist and a timeline for your health-related preparations. The *Country Information Worksheet* will help you and your doctor identify any special medical preparations which your travels may require. It will also make it easier to obtain emergency medical attention overseas if it becomes necessary. The *Medical Kit Checklist* will help you pack the the medications and supplies which you will want to take with you on your travels. The *Medical Documents Checklist* will help you collect all of the important medical documents which you should carry with you. Finally, the *Emergency Information Worksheet* will assemble in one place all of the critical information you or your contact person at home will need in the event of an unanticipated emergency.

These forms include basic items of information which all travelers will find helpful. No standard form will be perfect for everyone, so customize these forms by adding any information which is apppropriate for your health and travel plans and by making as many notes on them as you find useful.

Photocopy these forms and use them each time you travel. These worksheets and checklists are also available in full-sized, reproducible form from the publisher for the cost of postage and handling. Use the order form at the back of this book to order your set.

Finally, use these forms. They will make your preparations and travels easier and less stressful. There is an enormous security in knowing that you have done everything you should have and packed everything you will need. And, if an emergency does occur, having this information conveniently at your fingertips may contribute to a successful treatment and recovery.

TRIP PLANNING CHECKLIST

TIME	*ACTIVITY*

2 months   ☐ Itinerary
- *What countries*
- *What order*
- *Dates*
- *Activities (off tourist route?)*

☐ Medical checkup
- *Routine exam*
- *Chronic problems*
- *Special tests*
- *Discuss travel plans/precautions*
- *Medications, copies of prescriptions*
- *Written health history*

☐ Dental checkup

5 weeks   ☐ Determine immunization and antimalaria drug requirements

4 weeks   ☐ Immunizations

3 weeks   ☐ Antimalaria drugs (if needed)

☐ Traveler's insurance

☐ Contact IAMAT or other organization for sources of medical help abroad

2 weeks   ☐ Medical kit

☐ Country Information Worksheet
- *Doctors*
- *Embassies*

☐ Medical Document Checklist

☐ Select contact person at home

☐ Emergency Information Worksheet

Anytime   ☐ First Aid course

☐ CPR Course

<u>NOTES</u>:

COUNTRY INFORMATION
WORKSHEET

COUNTRY

Risk Level: _____

Dates of visit: ____/____/____ to ____/____/____

PLANNED ACTIVITIES

(for assessing level of health risk)

IMMUNIZATIONS REQUIRED

MALARIA REGIMEN

Date to begin malaria regimen _____/____/____

Date to end malaria regimen _____/____/____

U.S. EMBASSY OR
FOREIGN SERVICE OFFICES

Address

Phone

Address

Phone

Address

Phone

CANADIAN EMBASSY OR HIGH COMMISSION OFFICE

Address

Phone

PHYSICIANS AND HOSPITALS

(From IAMAT or Other Sources)

Name

Address

Phone

Specialty

Name

Address

Phone

Specialty

Name

Address

Phone

Specialty

LOCAL CONTACTS

NOTES

MEDICAL KIT CHECKLIST

Risk Level I

- ☐ Adhesive bandages (bandaids)
- ☐ Adhesive tape
- ☐ Moleskin (for blisters)
- ☐ Ace bandage
- ☐ Cotton swabs
- ☐ Scissors
- ☐ Tweezers
- ☐ Nail clippers and/or nail scissors
- ☐ Safety pins
- ☐ Pen knife
- ☐ Condoms, diaphragm, spermicide
  for sexually active travelers
- ☐ Tampons, sanitary napkins (for women)
- ☐ Eyeglasses or contact lenses, including extra pair
- ☐ Aspirin, acetaminophen, or ibuprofen
- ☐ Lip balm (preferably with sunscreen)
- ☐ Sunscreen, SPF 15 or higher as appropriate
- ☐ Skin cream
- ☐ Baby powder or medicated powder
  (for heat rash)
- ☐ Insect repellent containing deet
- ☐ Motion sickness medication (if needed)

Risk Level II

A complete Risk Level I kit, plus:

- ☐ Thermometer in hard case
- ☐ Gauze pads
- ☐ Bulb syringe (for irrigating wounds, etc.)
- ☐ Contact lens cleaning solution
- ☐ Antibiotic ointment
- ☐ Disinfectant soap (Dial® or Betadine®)

- ☐ Antihistamine or decongestant
- ☐ Strong pain killer
- ☐ Eye drops
- ☐ Pepto-Bismol® for mild diarrhea (tablets or liquid)
- ☐ Oil of cloves for dental problems
- ☐ Water purification tablets
- ☐ Immersion coil and adaptor for boiling water

Risk Level III

A complete Risk Level II kit, plus:

- ☐ First aid manual
- ☐ Fluid replacement formula
- ☐ Sterile syringes and needles
  (if traveling to a place with poor hygiene practices)
- ☐ Physician's note authorizing syringes and needles

If you are going off the normal tourist route:

- ☐ Antibiotics
- ☐ Physician's prescription for antibiotics
- ☐ Metronidazole (Flagyl®) for parasitic infections
- ☐ Physician's prescription for metronidazole
- ☐ Lindane (Kwell®) for lice
- ☐ Physician's prescription for Lindane

Prescription Drugs

Personal medications, including copies of prescriptions using generic names:

- ☐
- ☐
- ☐
- ☐
- ☐
- ☐

Additional prescription drugs when indicated
(including copies of prescriptions)

- ☐ Antimalaria drugs (Level III)
- ☐ Scopolamine patch for motion sickness,
  if appropriate
- ☐ Diarrhea medicine (Levels II and III)
- ☐ Medicine for vaginal yeast, if appropriate
- ☐ Treatment for allergy to insect bites
- ☐ Acetazolamide (Diamox®) for mountain sickness
- ☐
- ☐
- ☐
- ☐
- ☐

For travelers with young children:

- ☐ Syrup of ipecac (in case of accidental poisoning)
- ☐ Fluid replacement formula
  or Oral Rehydration Formula
- ☐ Ear drops and antibiotics, if needed.
- ☐ Insect repellent with lower concentration
  of deet (n,n-diethyl-meta-toluamide)
- ☐ Chewable antihistamine (such as Benadryl®)
  for allergic reactions
- ☐ Nose aspirator
- ☐ Ear wax drops
- ☐ Disposable wipes
- ☐ Sunscreen
- ☐ Childproof locks and outlet covers
- ☐ Child's prescription medications, especially if
  prone to ear infections. (including copies of
  prescriptions)
- ☐
- ☐
- ☐
- ☐

NOTE: Additional supplies are needed for travelers with special needs, including pregnant women, diabetics, and others with chronic medical problems. Consult your physician if you have health conditions which require special medications or treatments.

Other Medical Supplies:

☐
☐
☐
☐
☐
☐
☐
☐

Notes:

MEDICAL DOCUMENT CHECKLIST

☐ Medical history summary (several copies),
  written by your doctor and describing:
  - *Medical problems*
  - *Generic names for prescription drugs
    and reasons for prescribing*
  - *allergies*
  - *restrictions on immunizations*

☐ Test results (where appropriate):
  - *EKG*
  - *Chest X-ray*
  - *TB skin test*
  - *HIV antibody test*

☐ Immunization certificate

☐ Copies of prescriptions for drugs,
  using generic and brand names

☐ Copies of prescriptions for corrective lenses

☐ Your doctor's name, address, and phone number

☐ MedicAlert tag, bracelet, or wallet card

☐ Travel insurance claim forms
  and hotline number

☐ Country Information Worksheets
  for each country, including:
  - *U.S. and Canadian Embassy phone numbers*
  - *Names, addresses, and phone numbers
    of doctors or hospitals at each destination*

☐ Contact numbers for travelers'
  organizations, such as IAMAT

☐ Contact person's name, address, and phone number

☐ *The Travel Health™ Clinic
  Pocket Guide To Healthy Travel*

EMERGENCY INFORMATION CHECKLIST

The following information should be assembled and given to your contact person at home whenever you travel overseas. Make a copy and carry it with you as well, so that you know the information your contact person has received.

☐ Names, addresses, and phone numbers of people to contact in an emergency
- *Doctor*
- *Lawyer*
- *Travel insurance agent or carrier*
- *Close relatives*
- *Other emergency numbers*
  Overseas Citizens Emergency Center
  (202-647-5225)

☐ Itinerary Information
- *Flight information*
- *Hotels and other lodging*
- *Copies of Country Information Worksheets*

☐ Health-related documents
- *Copies of all medical documents*
  Medical history
  Test results
  Immunization records
  Prescriptions
- *Copy of insurance policy or policy number*

☐ Other papers (optional)
  · *Bank account number*
  · *Power of attorney*

Notes:

Appendix B

COUNTRY INFORMATION

This appendix is a country-by-country compilation of the addresses and phone numbers of American foreign service outposts and Canadian diplomatic and consular missions in a large number of traveler's destinations. It also lists the Risk Level of each nation included.

Use this information while you are planning your trip. Addresses and phone numbers should be added to your Country Information Worksheets so that the data will be at your fingertips. Risk Level references can help you and your doctor make your medical preparations.

This information is accurate as of the time when this book went to press. Addresses, phone numbers, and risk levels are subject to change, so it is always a good idea to verify the accuracy of your information before plans become final.

Country	Risk Level	American Foreign Service	Canadian Representation
AFGHANISTAN	III	None	
ALBANIA	II	Rruga Labinoti 103, **Tirana** (32875)	Contact Serbia and Montenegro
ALGERIA	III	4 Chemin Cheich Bachir El-Ibrahimi, **Algiers** (601-425/255/186) 14 Square de Bamako, **Oran** (334-509, 335-499) (Saturday-Wednesday)	27 Bis Rue Ali Massoudi, **Hydra** (60-66-11)
AMERICAN SAMOA	II	U.S. Territory	None
ANGOLA	III	None	Rua Rei Katyavalla 113, **Luanda** (34-37-54)

Country	Risk Level	American Foreign Service	Canadian Representation
ANTIGUA AND BARBUDA	II	Queen Elizabeth Hwy, **St. Johns** (462-3505)	Contact Barbados
ARGENTINA	II	4300 Colombia, **Buenos Aires** (774-7611/8811/9911)	2828 Tagle, 1425 **Buenos Aires** (805-3032)
ARMENIA	II	18 General Bagramian St., **Yerevan** (15-11-44)	Contact Russia
ARUBA	II	Contact Curacao	
AUSTRALIA	I	Moonah Pl., **Canberra** (270-5000) 533 St. Kilda Rd., **Melbourne** (526-5900) Pacific Power Bldg, 36th Fl., Hyde Park Square, Park & Elizabeth Sts., **Sydney** (261-9200) 383 Wickhamler Ter., 4th Floor, **Brisbane** (405-5555) 16 St. George's Ter., 13th Floor, **Perth** (231-9400) State Bank Centre, 91 King William St., Level 24, **Adelaide** (233-5819)	Commonwealth Ave., **Canberra** (273-3844) Level 5, Quay West Bldg., 111 Harrington St., **Sydney** (364-3000) 6th Floor, 1 Collins St., **Melbourne** (654-1433) 11th Floor, National Mutual Centre, 111 St. George's Ter., **Perth** (322-7930)
AUSTRIA	I	Boltzmanngasse 16, **Vienna** (31-339) Giselakai 51, **Salzburg** (28-6-01)	Schubertring 10, **Vienna** (533-3691...95, 533-6626...28)
AZERBAIJAN	III	83 Azadlig, **Baku** (96-00-19)	Contact Russia
AZORES	II	Avenida D. Henrique, Ponta Delgada, **Sao Miguel** (22216...19)	
BAHAMAS	II	Mosmar Bldg., Queen St., **Nassau** (322-1181/328-2206)	Out Island Traders Building, Office 21, **Nassau** (393-2123/2124/1305)

Country	Risk Level	American Foreign Service	Canadian Representation
BAHRAIN	III	Bldg. 979, Road No. 3119, Zinj District, **Manama** (973-273-300) (Saturday-Wednesday)	Contact Kuwait
BANGLADESH	III	Diplomatic Enclave, Madani Ave., Baridhara, **Dhaka** (88-4700/22)	House CWN 16/A, Road 48, Gulshan, **Dhaka** (88-36-39)
BARBADOS	II	Canadian Imperial Bank of Commerce Bldg., Broad St., **Bridgetown** (436-4950) American Life Insuranced Company Bldg., **Cheapside** (431-0225)	Bishops Court Hill, St Michael, **Bridgetown** (429-3550)
BELARUS	II	46 Starovilenskaya Ulitsa, **Minsk** (34-65-37/31-50-00)	Contact Russia
BELGIUM	I	27 Boulevard du Regent, B-1000, **Brussels** (513-38-30) Rubens Center, Nationalestraat 5, B-2000, **Antwerp** (321-8000)	2 avenue de Tervuren, **Brussels** (735-60-40)
BELIZE	III	Gabourel Lane and Hutson St., **Belize City** (77-161)	85 North St., **Belize City** (31-060)
BENIN	III	Rue Caporal Anani Bernard, **Cotonou** (30-06-50, 30-05-13, 30-17-92)	Contact Ghana
BERMUDA	II	Crown Hill, 16 Middle Rd., Devonshire, **Hamilton** (295-1342)	Contact New York
BHUTAN	III	None	None

Country	Risk Level	American Foreign Service	Canadian Representation
BOLIVIA	III	Banco Popular del Peru Bldg., Corner of Calles Mercado & Colon, **La Paz** (350-251) Edificio Oriente on Calle Bolivian, corner of Chuquisaca, Rm. 311, **Santa Cruz** (330-725, 325-544) Avenida Libertador Bolivar 1724 (Cala Cala), **Cochambamba** (43-216)	Avenida 20 de Octubre 2475, Plaza Avaroa, Sopocach, **La Paz** (37-52-24)
BOSNIA-HERZEGOVINA	II	Contact Serbia and Montenegro or Croatia	Contact Serbia and Montenegro
BOTSWANA	III	P.O. Box 90, **Gaborone** (35-39-82)	No. 1, Equity Bldg., The Mall, **Gaborone** (31-43-77)
BRAZIL	III	Avenida das Nocoes, Lote 3, **Brasilia** (321-7272) Avenida Presidente Wilson 147, **Rio De Janeiro** (292-7117) Rua Padre Joao Manoel 933, **Sao Paulo** (881-6511) Rua Coronel Genuino 421, 9th Floor, **Porto Alegre** (221-1412) Rua Goncalves Maia 163, **Recife** (221-1412) Avenida Presidente Antonio Carlos Magalhaes S/N Edificio Cidadella Center, Suite 410, Candeal, **Salvador Da Bahia** (358-9195) Avenida Oswaldo Cruz 165, **Belem** (223-0800/0413)	Setor de Embaixadas Sul, Avenida das Nocoes lote 16, **Brasilia** (321-2171) Edificio Top Center, Avenida Paulista 854, 5th Floor, **Sao Paulo** (287-2122/2234/2213, 285-3217/3240) Rua Lauro Muller, 116, Sala 1104-Torre Rio Sul-Botafogo, 22290 **Rio de Janeiro** (275-2137)

Country	Risk Level	American Foreign Service	Canadian Representation
BRAZIL (Cont.)		Rua Recife 1010, Adrianopolis, **Manaos** (234-4546) Instituto Brasiz-Estados Unidos, Rua Nogueira Acioly, 891, Aldeota, **Fortaleza** (252-1539)	
BRUNEI DARUSSALAM	II	3rd Floor, Teck Guan Plaza, Jalan Sultan, **Bandar Seri Begawan** (229-670)	Contact Singapore
BULGARIA	II	1 Suborna, **Sofia** (88-48-01...05)	Contact Serbia and Montenegro
BURKINA FASO	III	P. O. Box 35, **Ouagadougou** (30-67-23...25)	Canadian Development Centre, **Ouagadougou** (31-18-94...97, 31-25-85)
BURUNDI	III	Avenue des Etats-Unis, **Bujumbura** (454)	Contact Zaire
CAMEROON	III	Rue Nachtigal, B.P. 817, **Yaounde** (234014) 21 Ave. du General De Gaulle, **Douala** (425331, 420303)	Immeuble Stamatiades, Place de 'Hotel de Ville, **Yaounde** (23-02-03, 22-19-36, 22-18-22, 22-16-90, 23-23-11)
CANADA	I	360 University Ave., **Toronto** (416-595-1700) 1095 W. Pender St., **Vancouver** (604-685-4311) 100 Wellington St., **Ottawa** (613-238-5335) Room 1050, 615 Macleod Trail S.E., **Calgary** (403-266-8962) Suite 910, Cogswell Tower, Scotia Square, **Halifax** (902-429-2480) 1155 St. Alexander St., **Montreal** (514-398-9695) 2 Place Terrasse Dufferin, **Quebec** (418-692-2095)	

Country	Risk Level	American Foreign Service	Canadian Representation
CANARY ISLANDS	II	None	None
CAPE VERDE	III	1st and 3rd Floors, Rua Hoji Ya Yenna 81, **Praia** (553, 761)	Contact Senegal
CAYMAN ISLANDS	II	George Town, **Grand Cayman** (809-949-8440); also contact Kingston, Jamaica	None
CENTRAL AFRICAN REPUBLIC	III	Avenue David Dacko, **Bangui** (61-02-00, 61-25-78, 61-43-33, 61-02-10)	Contact Cameroon
CHAD	III	Ave. Felix Ebove, **N'djamena** (62-18, 40-09, 62-11)	Contact Cameroon
CHILE	II	Codina Bldg., 1343 Agustinas, **Santiago** (671-0133)	Ahumada 11, 10th Floor, **Santiago** (692-2256...59)
CHINA, PEOPLE'S REPUBLIC OF	III	Xiu Shui Dong Jie 3, **Beijing** (532-3831) No. 1 South Shamian St., Shamina Island 20031, **Guangzhou** (888-8911, ext. 255) 1469 Huai Hai Middle Rd., **Shanghai** (433-6880) No. 40 Lane 4, Section 5, Sanjing St. Heping Dist., **Shenyang** (220000) Jinjiang Hotel, 180 Renmin Rd., **Chengdu** (582222, ext. 131)	19 Dong Zhi Men Wai St., **Beijing** (532-3536) Shanghai American International Centre at Shanghai Centre, West Tower, Ste 604, 1376 Nanjing Xi Lu, **Shanghai** 200040 (279-8400)
CHRISTMAS ISLAND	II	None	None
COLOMBIA	III	Calle 38, No. 8-61, **Bogota** (320-1300)	Calle 76, No. 11-52, **Bogota** (217-5555)

Country	Risk Level	American Foreign Service	Canadian Representation
COLOMBIA (Cont.)		Calle 77, Carrera 68, Centro Comercial Mayorista, **Barranquilla** (457-088)	Calle de la Inquisicion con, Santo Domingo Esquina No 33-08, Apartamento 201, **Cartagena** (647-393)
COMOROS	III	Boite Pastale (B.P. 1318), **Moroni** (73-22-03, 73-29-22)	Contact Kenya
CONGO, PEOPLE'S REPUBLIC OF THE	III	Avenue Amilcar Cabral, **Brazzaville** (83-20-70)	Contact Zaire
COOK ISLANDS	II	None	None
COSTA RICA	III	Pavas, **San Jose** (20-39-39, 20-31-27)	6th Floor, Cronos Building, Calle 3 & Ave. Central, **San Jose** (55-35-22)
CROATIA	III	Andrije Hebranga 2, **Zagreb** (444-800)	Mihanoviceva 1, **Zagreb** (42-87-83, 43-56-66, ext.111)
CUBA	II	Swiss Embassy, Calcado entre L & M, Vedado Section, **Havana** (33-3550...59)	Calle 30, No. 518 Esquina a7a, Miramar, **Havana** (33-25-16/17/27, 33-23-82, 33-27-52)
CURACAO	II	J.B. Gorsiraweg # 1, **Willemstad** (613-066)	Maduro and Curiels Bank, N.V., Plaza JoJo Corres 2-4, **Willemstad** (61-35-15)
CYPRUS	II	Metochiou and Ploutarchou Street, Engomi, **Nicosia** (467100)	15 Themistocles Dervis St., Margarita House, Ste. 403, **Nicosia** (45-16-30)
CZECH REPUBLIC	II	Trziste 15, **Prague** (536-641, 536-646)	Mickiewiczova 6, 125 33 **Prague** (312-0251...55)

Country	Risk Level	American Foreign Service	Canadian Representation
DENMARK	I	Dag Hammarskjold Alle 24, Copenhagen (01-42-31-44)	Kr. Bernikowsgade 1, 1105 Copenhagen (12-22-99)
DJIBOUTI	III	Plateau du Serpent, Boulevard Marechal Joffre, Djibouti City (35-39-95) (Sunday-Thursday)	Contact Ethiopia
DOMINICA	II	Contact Barbados	Contact Barbados
DOMINICAN REPUBLIC	III	Corner of Calle Cesar Nicolas Penson & Calle Leopoldo Navarro, Santo Domingo (809-541-2171)	Maximo Gomez 30, Santo Domingo (698-0002) Beller 51, Ste. 3, Puerto Plata (586-5761/3305)
ECUADOR	III	Avenida 12 de Octubre y Avenida Patria, Quito (562-890, 561-749) 9 de Octubre y Garcia Moreno, Guayaquil (323-570, 327-893)	Edificio Josueth Gonzalez, Ave. Sais de Diciembre 2816 y James Orton, Piso 4, Quito (564-795, 506-162/163) General Cordova 802 y Victor Manuel Rendon, Edificio torres de la Merced, Piso 21, Oficina 6, Guayaquil (31-37-47, 30-35-80)
EGYPT	III	Lazoghli St., Garden City, Cairo (355-7371) 110 Ave. Horreya, Sharqia Dist., Alexandria (482-1911, 482-1848)	6 Mohammed Fahmiel El Sayed St., Garden City, Cairo (354-3110)
EL SALVADOR	III	Final Blvd. Santa Elena, Urbanization Santa Elena, Antigua Cuscatlan, San Salvador (78-4444)	111 Avenida Las Palmas, Colonia San Benito, San Salvador (74-49-93)
ENGLAND	I	24/31 Grosvenor Sq., London (499-9000)	MacDonald House, 1 Grosvenor Sq, London (658-6600)

Country	Risk Level	American Foreign Service	Canadian Representation
EQUATORIAL GUINEA	III	Calle de Los Ministros, **Malabo** (2406)	Contact Gabon
ESTONIA	II	Kentmanni 20, **Tallinn** (312-021...24, 312-024)	Contact Finland
ETHIOPIA	III	Entoto St., **Addis Ababa** (555-666, ext 316/336, 552-558)	African Solidarity Insurance Bldg., 6th Floor, Churchill Ave., **Addis Ababa** (51-13-43, 51-12-28, 51-13-19, 51-11-00)
FALKLAND ISLANDS	II	None	None
FIJI	II	31 Loftus St., **Suva** (314-466, 314-069)	L.I.C.I. Bldg., 7th Floor, Butt St., **Suva** (30-05-89)
FINLAND	I	Itainen Puistotie 14A, **Helsinki** (17-19-31)	P. Esplanadi 25B, **Helsinki** (17-11-41)
FRANCE	I	2 Avenue Gabriel, **Paris** (4296-1202) 22 Cours du Marechal-Foch, **Bordeaux** (52-6595) 7 Quai General-Sarrail, **Lyon** (824-68-49) 12 Boulevard Paul Peytral, **Marseilles** (54-9200) 1 Rue du Marechal Joffre, **Nice** (88-8955) 15 Avenue d'Alsace, **Strasbourg** (35-3104)	35, avenue Montaigne, **Paris** (44-43-32-00)
FRENCH ANTILLES	II	Contact Martinique	
FRENCH GUIANA	III	Contact Martinique	
FRENCH POLY-NESIA (TAHITI)	II	Contact Fiji	

Country	Risk Level	American Foreign Service	Canadian Representation
GABON	III	Blvd. de la Mer, P.O. Box 4000, **Libreville** (762003/4, 743492)	P.O. Box 4037, **Libreville** (74-34-64/65)
GAMBIA	III	Fajara (East), Pipeline Rd., **Serrekanda** (93-2856, 93-2858)	See Senegal
GEORGIA	II	25 Atoneli St., **Tbilisi** (98-99-67/68)	See Russia
GERMANY	I	Neustaedtische Kirchstrasse 4-5, **Berlin** (238-5174) Clayallee 179, **Berlin** (819-7465/66) Deichmanns Aue 29, **Bonn** (339) Siesmayerstrasse 21, **Frankfurt** (75350) Alsterufer 27/28, **Hamburg** (411710) Koeniginstrasse 5, **Munich** (2888-0) Urbanstrasse 7, **Stuttgart** (21450) Wilhelm-Seyfferth-Strasse 4, **Leipzig** (211-7866)	Friedrich Wilhelm Strasse 18, **Bonn** (968-0) Friedrichstr. 95, **Berlin** (261-1161...63) Immermannstrasse 65D, **Dusseldorf** (35-34-71) 3rd Floor, Tal 29, D-8000, Munich (22-26-61)
GHANA	III	Ring Road, East, **Accra** (77-53-47)	42 Independence Ave., **Accra** (77-37-61,22-85-55/66)
GIBRALTAR	II	None	None
GILBERT ISLANDS	II	None	None
GREECE	II	91 Vasilissis Sophias Blvd., **Athens** (721-2951, 721-8401)	4 Ioannou Gennadiou St., **Athens** (723-9511...19)

Country	Risk Level	American Foreign Service	Canadian Representation
GREENLAND	I	None	Groenlandsfly A/S Nuuk (28888)
GRENADA	II	**St. George's** (444-1173)	Contact Barbados
GUADELOUPE	II	None	None
GUAM	II	U.S. Territory	None
GUATEMALA	III	Avenida de la Reforma 7-01, Zone 10, **Guatemala City** (31-15-41)	13 Calle 8-44, zona 10, Edyma Plaza, **Guatemala City** (33-61-02)
GUERNSEY, ALDERNEY, AND SARK	· I	None	None
GUINEA	III	2nd Blvd & 9th Ave., **Conakry** (415-20...24)	P.O. Box 99, **Conakry** (44-23-95)
GUINEA-BISSAU	III	Avenida Domingos Ramos, **Bissau** (20-1139/1145/0113)	Contact Senegal
GUYANA	III	99-100 Young and Duke Sts., Kingston, **Georgetown** (54900/9, 57-963)	High & Young Streets, **Georgetown** (72081/5)
HAITI	III	Harry Truman Blvd., **Port-au-Prince** (22-0200/0354/0368/0612)	édifice Banque Nova Scotia, route de Delmas, **Port-au-Prince** (23-2358)
HONDURAS	III	Avenido La Paz, **Tegucigalpa** (32-3120...25)	Edificio Comercial Los Castanos, 6th Piso, Blvd. Morazan, **Tegucigalpa** (31-45-45/51)
HONG KONG	II	26 Garden Rd., **Hong Kong** (523-9011)	11-14th Floors, 1 Exchange Square, 8 Connaught Place, **Hong Kong** (810-4321)

Country	Risk Level	American Foreign Service	Canadian Representation
HUNGARY	II	V. Szabadsag Ter 12, **Budapest** (112-6450)	Budakeszi ut. 32, **Budapest** (1767-312/512/711/712)
ICELAND	I	Laufasvegur 21, **Reykjavik** (629100)	Sudurlandsbraut 10, **Reykjavik** (68-08-20)
INDIA	III	Shanti Path, Chanakyapuri 110021, **New Delhi** (600651) Lincoln House, 78 Bhulabhai Desai Rd. 400026, **Bombay** (363-3611) 5/1 Ho Chi Minh Sarani, **Calcutta** (22-3611...15, 22-2335...37) Mount Rd., **Madras** (473-040/477-542)	7/8 Shantipath, Chanakyapuri, **New Delhi** (687-6500) 41/42 Maker Chambers VI, K° Jamnalai Bajaj Marg, Nariman Point, **Bombay** (287-6027...30/5479)
INDONESIA	III	Medan Merdeka Selatan 5, **Jakarta** (360-360) Jalan Imam Bonjol 13, **Medan** (322200) Jalan Raya Dr. Sutomo 33, **Surabaya** (582-287/8) Janal Segara Ayu No. 5, **Sanur Bali** (88478, 88978)	5th Floor, WISMA Metropolitan, Jalan Jendral Sudirman, **Jakarta** (51-07-09)
IRAN	III	None	57 Shahid Javad-e-Sarfaraz (Daryaye-Noor), Ostad-Motahari Ave., **Tehran** (62-26-23)
IRAQ	III	Polish Embassy, opposite Foreign Ministry Club (Masbah Quarter), **Baghdad** (719-6138/9, 719-3791, 718-1840)	Hay Al Mansour, Mahalla 609, St. 1, House 33, **Baghdad** (542-1459/1932/1933)
IRELAND	I	42 Elgin Rd., Ballsbridge, **Dublin** (688-7777)	65 St. Stephen's Green, **Dublin** (78-19-88)

Country	Risk Level	American Foreign Service	Canadian Representation
ISRAEL	II	71 Hayarkon St., **Tel Aviv** (517-4338) 27 Nablus Rd., **Jerusalem** (253-288, 253-201) 12 Jerusalem St., **Haifa** (670-616)	220 Rehov Hayarkon, **Tel Aviv** (527-2929)
ITALY	II	Via Veneto 119/A, **Rome** (46741) Via Principe Amedeo 2/10, **Milan** (290-341) Lungarmo Amerigo Vespucci 38, **Florence** (239-8276...78, 217-605) Via Roma 15, **Trieste** (660177)	Via G.B. de Rossi 27, **Rome** (841-5341) Via Vittor Pisani 19, **Milan** (310368)
IVORY COAST	III	5 Rue Jesse Owens, **Abidjan** (21-09-79)	Immeuble Trade Center, 23 Ave. Nogues, Le Plateau, **Abidjan** (32-20-09)
JAMAICA	II	Jamaica Mutual Life Center, 2 Oxford Rd., 3rd Floor, **Kingston** (929-4850...59) St. James Place, 2nd Floor, Gloucester Ave., **Montego Bay** (809-952-0160/5050)	Mutual Security Ban Building, 30-36 Knutsford Blvd., **Kingston** (926-1500...07) 29 Gloucester St., **Montego Bay** (952-6198)
JAPAN	I II (Rural)	10-5, Akasaka 1-chome, Minato-ku, **Tokyo** (3-224-5000) 2564 Nishihara, Urasoe, Naha, **Okinawa** (876-4211) 5-26 Ohori 2-chome, Chuo-ku, **Fukuoka** (751-9331/4) Kita 1-jo Nishi 28-chome, Chuo-ku, **Sapporo** (641-1115) 11-5 Nishitenma 2-chome, Kita-ku, **Osaka** (315-5900)	3-38 Akasaka 7-chome, Minato-ku, **Tokyo** (3408-2101) Daisan Shoho Bldg., 12th Floor, 2-2-3 Nishi-Shinsaibashi, Chuo-ku, **Osaka** (212-4910) ET Building, A-9th Floor, No. 8-28, Watanabe Dori, 4-chome, Chuo-ku, **Fukuoka** Nakato Marunouchi Bldg., 6F, 3-1-6 Marunouchi, Naku-ku, **Nagoya** (972-0450)

Country	Risk Level	American Foreign Service	Canadian Representation
JORDAN	III	Jebel Amman, **Amman** (443716) (Sunday-Thursday)	Pearl of Shmeisani Building, Shmeisani, **Amman** (66-61-24...26)
KAMPUCHEA (CAMBODIA)	III	None	None
KAZAKHSTAN	III	99/97 Furmanova St, **Almaty** (63-24-26)	Contact Russia
KENYA	III	Moi/Haile Selassie Avenue, **Nairobi** (334-141) Paili House, Nyerere Avenue, **Mombasa** (315-101)	Comcraft House, Haile Selassie Avenue, **Nairobi** 21-48-04)
KIRGHIZSTAN	III	Erkindik Prospect #66, **Bishkek** (22-26-93)	Contact Russia
KIRIBATI	II	None	Contact New Zealand
KOREA, DEMOCRATIC PEOPLE'S REPUBLIC OF, (NORTH KOREA)	II	None	None
KOREA, REPUBLIC OF, (SOUTH KOREA)	II	82 Sejong-Ro, Chongro-ku, **Seoul** (1392-4000/4008, 397-4114)	Kolon Building, 10th Floor, 45 Mugyo-Dong; Jung-Ku, **Seoul** (753-2605...08/7290...93)
KUWAIT	II	P.O. Box 77 SAFAT, **Kuwait City** (242-4151...59) (Sunday-Thursday)	Block 4, House No. 24, Al-Mutawakei, **Da Aiyah** (265-3025)
LAOS	III	Rue Bartholoni, **Vientiane** (2220, 2357, 2384, 3570)	Contact Thailand
LATVIA	II	Raina Blvd., **Riga** (210-005)	Contact Sweden

Country	Risk Level	American Foreign Service	Canadian Representation
LEBANON	II	Antelias, **Beirut** (417-774, 415-802/803, 402-200, 403-300)	Contact Syria
LESOTHO	II	P.O. Box 333, Maseru 100, **Maseru** (312-666)	5 Orpen Rd., **Maseru** (32-41-89)
LIBERIA	III	111 United Nations Dr., **Monrovia** (222991...94)	EXCHEM Compound, Harbel, **Monrovia** (223-903)
LIBYA	III	None	Contact Tunisia
LIECHTENSTEIN	II	None	None
LITHUANIA	II	Akmenu 6, **Vilnius** (22-30-31)	Contact Sweden
LUXEMBOURG	I	22 Blvd. Emmanuel-Servais, **Luxembourg City** (46-01-23)	c/o Price Waterhouse and Co., 24-26 ave. de la Liberte, **Luxembourg City** (40-24-20)
MACAO	II	None	Contact Hong Kong
MACEDONIA	II	Contact Bulgaria or Serbia and Montenegro	Contact Serbia and Montenegro
MADAGASCAR	III	14 & 16 Rue Rainitovo, Antsahavola, **Antananarivo** (212-57, 200-89, 207-18)	c/o QIT-Madagascar Minerals, Lot II-J-169 Vila 3H Ivandry, **Antananarivo** (425-59)
MADEIRA	II	Avenida Luis de Camoes, **Funchal** (743-429)	None
MALAWI	III	Area 40, Center City, **Lilongwe** (783-166/342)	**Lilongwe** (72-37-32)
MALAYSIA	III	376 Jalan Tun Razak, **Kuala Lumpur** (248-9011)	7th Floor, Plaza MBF, 172 Jalan Ampang, 5th Fl., **Kuala Lumpur** (261-2000)

Country	Risk Level	American Foreign Service	Canadian Representation
MALDIVES, REPUBLIC OF	III	Mandhu Edurruge, 20-05 Violet Magu, **Male** (322581, 325199); Also contact Sri Lanka	Contact Sri Lanka
MALI	III	Rue Rochester NY & Rue Mohammed V, **Bamako** (22-54-70)	**Bamako** (22-22-36)
MALTA	II	3rd Floor, Development House, St. Anne St., Floriana, **Valletta** (235-960)	Demajo House, 103 Archbishop St., **Valletta** (233-121)
MARSHALL ISLANDS	II	Near Mormon church and "Blue Wall" compound, **Majuro** (247-4011)	None
MARTINIQUE	II	14 Rue Blenac, **Fort-de-France** (63-13-03)	None
MAURITANIA	III	Between Presidency Bldg. and Spanish Embassy, **Nouakchott** (526-60)	Contact Senegal
MAURITIUS	III	Rogers House, 4th Floor, John Kennedy St., **Port-Louis** (208-9763...67)	Contact Tanzania
MEXICO	III	Paseo de la Reforma 305, Colonia Cuauhtemoc, **Mexico City** (211-0042) Progreso 175, **Guadalajara** (25-2998) Avenida Monterrey 141, **Hermosillo** (172375) Avenida Constitucion 411 Poniente, **Monterrey** (45-2120) Tapachula 96, **Tijuana** (817400)	Calle Schiller No. 529 (Rincon del Bosque), Colonia Polanco, **Mexico City** (724-7900) Hotel Club del Sol, Costera Miguel Aleman esq. Reyes Catolicos, **Acapulco** (566-21/00, ext. 7347) Hotel Playa Mazatlan, Zona Dorada Rodolfo Loaiza 202, **Mazatlan** (13-73-20, 13-44-44, ext. 370)

Country	Risk Level	American Foreign Service	Canadian Representation
MEXICO (Cont.)		924-N Avenida Lopez Mateos, **Ciudad Juarez** (134048) Ave. Primera No. 2002, **Matamoros** (6-72-70) Paseo Montejo 453, **Merida** (25-6366) Calle Allende 3330, Col. Jardin, **Nuevo Laredo** (4-0512)	German Gedovious 5-201, Condominio del Parque, **Tijuana** (84-04-61) Centro Comercial Plaza Mexico, Local 312, Ave. Tulum 200, esq. Agua, **Cancun** (437-16) Hotel Fiesta Americana, Local 30-A, Aurelio Aceves 225, **Guadalajara** (15-86-65, 25-34-34, ext. 3005) 119 Dr. Liceaga No. 8, **Oaxaca** (33777) Calle Hidalgo 226, **Puerto Vallarta** (253-98/17)
MICRONESIA	III	Lower Pics area across from Agriculture Station, **Kolonia** (320-2187)	None
MOLDOVA	III	Strada Alexei Mateevici 103, **Chisinau** (23-37-72)	Contact Romania
MONACO	II	Contact Marseilles or Nice, France	2 Honore Labande, Immeubles les Ligures, **Monte Carlo** (92-16-14-15
MONGOLIA	II	Micro Region 11, Big Ring Rd., **Ulaanbaatar** (329-095/606)	Contact Beijing, China
MONTSERRAT	II	None	None
MOROCCO	III	2 Ave. de Marrakech, **Rabat** (76-22-65) 8 Blvd. Moulay Youssef, **Casablanca** (26-45-50)	13 Bis, Rue Jaafar As-Sadik, **Rabat-Agdal** (77-28-80)
MOZAMBIQUE	III	193 Avenida Kenneth Kaunda, **Maputo** (49-27-97, 449-00-71)	22 Joaquim Lapa, 4th Floor, Rm. 4, **Maputo** (42-08-18)

Country	Risk Level	American Foreign Service	Canadian Representation
MYANMAR (BURMA)	III	581 Merchant St., Rangoon (82055, 82181)	Contact Bangladesh
NAMIBIA	III	14 Lossen St., Windhoek (221-675, 222-680)	111-A Gloudina St., Ludwigsdorf, Windhoek (22-29-66/41)
NAURU	II	Contact Fiji	None
NEPAL	III	Pani Pokhari, Kathmandu (411-179/613, 412-718, 413-890)	Contact New Delhi, India
NETHERLANDS	I	Lange Voorhout 102, The Hague (310-9209) Museumplein 19, Amsterdam (575-5309)	Sophialaan 7, The Hague (361-4111)
NETHERLANDS ANTILLES	II	Contact Curacao	Contact Curacao
NEW CALEDONIA	II	None	None
NEW ZEALAND	I	29 Fitzherbert Ter., Thorndon, Wellington (472-2068) 4th Floor, Yorkshire General Bldg., Shortland & O'Connell Sts., Auckland (303-2724) c/o Price Waterhouse Center, 119 Armagh St., Christchurch (379-0040)	61 Molesworth Street, Thorndon, Wellington (473-9577) Princes Court, 2 Princes St., Auckland (309-3960)
NICARAGUA	III	Km. 4-1/2 Carretera Sur, Managua (66-6010)	208 Calle de Triunfo, Frente Plazoleta Telcor Central, Managua (62-30-09/08)
NIGER	III	Rue Des Ambassades, Niamey (72-26-61...64)	Sonara II Bldg., ave. du Premier Pont, Niamey (73-36-86/87, 73-37-58)

Country	Risk Level	American Foreign Service	Canadian Representation
NIGERIA	III	2 Eleke Crescent, Victoria Island, **Lagos** (261-0097) 2 Maska Road, **Kaduna** (201-070)	Committee of Vice-Chancellors Building, Plot 8A, 4 Idowu-Taylor St., **Victoria Island** 269-2915...18) Plot no. 622, Cadastral Zone A5, Maitama, **Abuja** (same)
NIUE	II	None	None
NORTHERN IRELAND	I	14 Queen St., **Belfast** (328239)	Contact England
NORWAY	I	Drammensveien 18, Oslo 1, **Oslo** (44-85-50)	Oscar's Gate 20, **Oslo** (22-46-69-55)
OMAN	III	Safaraat St., Al-Khawair, **Muscat** (698-969, 699-049) (Saturday-Wednesday)	Flat No. 310, Bldg. 477, Way 2907, Moosa Abdul Rahman Hassan Bldg, A'Noor St. Ruwi, **Muscat** (791-738)
PACIFIC ISLANDS TRUST TERRITORY	II	U.S. Territory	None
PAKISTAN	III	Diplomatic Enclave, Ramna 5, **Islamabad** (826-161) 8 Abdullah Haroon Rd., **Karachi** (568-5170) Sharah-E-Abdul Hamid Bin Badees (50 Empress Rd.), New Simla Hills, **Lahore** (636-5530) 11 Hospital Road, **Peshawar** (279-801...03)	Diplomatic Enclave, Sector G-5, **Islamabad** (21-11-01) c/o Beach Luxury Hotel, Tamizuddin Khan Rd. Suite 336, **Karachi** (55-10-31)
PALAU, REPUBLIC OF	II	Koror (488-2920)	None

Country	Risk Level	American Foreign Service	Canadian Representation
PANAMA	III	Avenida Balboa y Calle 38, **Panama City** (27-17-77) Panama Agencies Bldg., Terminal and Pedro Prestan Sts., **Cristobal** (41-24-40/27-78)	Edificio Proconsa, Aero Peru Piso 5B, Calle Manuel y Caza, Campo Alegre, **Panama City** (64-70-14)
PAPUA NEW GUINEA	III	Armit St., **Port Moresby** (211-455/594/054)	2nd Floor, The Lodge, Brampton St., **Port Moresby** (21-35-99)
PARAGUAY	III	1776 Mariscal Lopez Ave. **Asuncion** (213-715)	El Paraguayo Independiente 995, Entrepiso, Oficinas 1 y 2. **Asuncion** (44-95-05, 49-17-30)
PERU	III	Corner Avenidas Inca Garcilaso de la Vega & Espana, **Lima** (33-8000) Grimaldo del Solar 346, Miraflores, **Lima** (44-3621/3121) Avenida Tullumayo 125, **Cuzco** (23-3541)	Federico Gerdes 130 (Ante Calle Libertad), Miraflores, **Lima** (44-40-15/44-38-41/44-38-93/44-39-20/44-39-40/44-46-88)
PHILIPPINES	III	1201 Roxas Blvd., **Manila** (521-7116) 3rd Floor, PCI Bank, Gorordo Ave., **Lahug,** Cebu (311-261)	Allied Bank Center, 9th and 11th Floors, 6754 Ayala Avenue, Makati, **Metro Manila** (815-9536)
PITCAIRN ISLAND	II	None	None
POLAND	II	Aleje Ujazdowskie 29/31, **Warsaw** (628-3041) Ulica Stolarska 9, **Krakow** (22-14-00) Ulica Chopina 4, **Poznan** (529-586)	Ulica Matejki 1/5, **Warsaw** (29-80-51/50/55/57/58)

Country	Risk Level	American Foreign Service	Canadian Representation
PORTUGAL	II	Avenida das Forcas Armadas, **Lisbon** (72-6600/8760/8880)	Avn. da Liberdade 144/56, 4th Floor, **Lisbon** (347-4892) Rua Frei Lourenco de Sta. Maria No. 1, 1st Floor, **Faro** (80-37-57, 80-30-00)
QATAR	II	149 Ali Bin Ahmed St., Farig Bin Omran, **Doha** (864-701...03) (Saturday–Wednesday)	Contact Kuwait
REUNION	II	None	None
ROMANIA	II	Strada Tudor Arghezi 7-9, **Bucharest** (312-4042/6386)	36 Nicolae Iorga, **Bucharest** (312-83-45/03-65)
RUSSIA	II	Novinskiy Bul'var 19/23, **Moscow** (252-2450, 252-1898, 255-5123) 12 Mordovtseva, **Vladivostok** (258-458, 266-734) Ulitsa Furshtadskaya 15, **St. Petersburg** (275-1701, 274-8692)	23 Starokonyushenny Pereulok, **Moscow** (241-1111/5070)
RWANDA	III	Blvd. de la Revolution, **Kigali** (75601...03)	**Kigali** (73210, 73278, 73787)
RYUKYU ISLANDS	II	None	None
SAINT KITTS AND NEVIS	II	Contact Antigua and Barbuda	Contact Barbados
SAINT HELENA	II	None	None
SAINT LUCIA	II	Contact Barbados	Contact Barbados

Country	Risk Level	American Foreign Service	Canadian Representation
SAINT VINCENT AND THE GRENADINES	II	Contact Barbados	Contact Barbados
SAMOA	II	None	None
SAN MARINO	II	None	Contact Rome, Italy
SAO TOME AND PRINCIPE	III	Contact Gabon	Contact Gabon
SAUDI ARABIA	III	Palestine Rd., Ruwais, **Jeddah** (02-667-0080) Between Aramco Headquarters and Dhahran International Airport, **Dhahran** (891-3200) Collector Rd. M, Riyadh Diplomatic Quarter, **Riyadh** (488-3800) (Saturday-Wednesday)	Diplomatic Quarter, **Riyadh** (488-2288/ 0275/0531/1221) Headquarters Bldg., Zahid Corporate Group, **Jeddah** (665-1050)
SCOTLAND	I	3 Regent Terr., **Edinburgh** (556-8315)	Contact England
SENEGAL	III	Avenue Jean XXIII, **Dakar** (23-42-96)	45 Ave. de la Republique, **Dakar** (23-92-90)
SERBIA AND MONTENEGRO	II	Kneza Milosa 50, **Belgrade** (64-64-81)	Kneze Milosa 75, **Belgrade** (64-46-66)
SEYCHELLES	II	Victoria House, 4th Floor, **Victoria** (25256)	Contact Tanzania
SIERRA LEONE	III	Corner Walpole & Siaka Stevens Sts., **Freetown** (226-481)	Contact Ghana
SINGAPORE	II	30 Hill Street, **Singapore** (338-0251)	80 Anson Rd., 14th and 15th Floors, IBM Towers, **Singapore** (223-6363)

Country	Risk Level	American Foreign Service	Canadian Representation
SLOVAK REPUBLIC	II	Hviezdoslavovo Namesti 4, **Bratislava** (330-861)	Contact Czech Republic
SLOVENIA	II	Prazakova 4, **Ljubljana** (310-427)	None
SOLOMON ISLANDS	III	Mud Alley, **Honiara** (23-890)	Contact Canberra, Australia
SOMALIA	III	Currently evacuated.	Contact Nairobi, Kenya
SOUTH AFRICA	II	Thibault House, 225 Pretorius St., **Pretoria** (28-4266) Broadway Industries Center, Heerengracht, Foreshore, **Cape Town** (214-280) Durban Bay House, 9th Floor, 333 Smith Street, **Durban** (304-4737) 11th Floor, Kine Center, Commissioner & Kruis Sts., **Johannesburg** (331-1681)	5th Floor, Nedbank Plaza, Corner Church and Beatgrtix Sts., Arcadia, **Pretoria** (342-3970/3978) 16th Floor, Reserve Bank Bldg., 30 Hout St., **Capetown** (23-5240, 24-5649 (January to June)
SPAIN	II	Serrano 75, **Madrid** (577-4000) Paseo Reina Elisenda 23-25, **Barcelona** (280-2777) Paseo de las Delicias 7, **Seville** (231-885) Lehendakari Agirre 11-3, **Bilbao** (475-8300) Centro Comercial "Las Rampas," Fase 2, Planta 1, Locales 12-g-7 and 12-G-8, Fuengirola, **Malaga** (474-891) Frachy y Roca 5-5', No. 13, **Las Palmas** (222-552) Cl. de La Paz 6-5, Local 5, **Valencia** (351-6973)	Edificio Goya, Calle Nunez de Balboa 35, **Madrid** (431-4300) Via Augusta 125, **Barcelona** (209-0634) Edificio Horizonte, Plaza de la Malagueta 3, **Malaga** (22-33-46) Avenida de la Constitucion 30, 2nd Floor, **Sevilla** (22-94-13)

Country	Risk Level	American Foreign Service	Canadian Representation
SPAIN (Cont.)		Av. Jamime 111 Entresuelo, 2-H-1 (97), **Palma de Mallorca** (725-051)	
SRI LANKA	III	201 Galle Road, Colombo 3, **Colombo** (448-007)	6 Gregory's Road, Cinnamon Gardens, **Colombo** (69-58-41...43, 69-87-97)
SUDAN	III	Sharia Ali Abdul Latif, **Khartoum** (74700, 74611)	Contact Addis Ababa, Ethiopia
SURINAME	III	Dr. Sophie Redmondstraat 129, **Paramaribo** (477-818)	Contact Guyana
SWAZILAND	III	Central Bank Bldg., Warner St., **Mbabane** (46441/5)	Contact Pretoria, South Africa
SWEDEN	I	Strandvagen 101, **Stockholm** (783-5300)	7th Floor, Tegelbacken 4, **Stockholm** (613-9900)
SWITZERLAND	I	Jubilaeumstrasse 93, **Berne** (437-011) Zollikerstrasse 141, **Zurich** (422-2566) Botanic Bldg., 1-3 Ave. de la Paix, **Geneva** (738-7613)	Kirchenfeldstrasse 88, **Berne** (44-63-81...5)
SYRIA	III	Abu Roumaneh, Al-Mansur St., No. 2, **Damascus** (33-3052/2557/0416/2814/2315/7178/3232, 71-4108)	Lot 12, Mezzeh Autostrade, **Damascus** (236-851/892)
TAIWAN (REPUBLIC OF CHINA)	II	American Institute in Taiwan, 7 Lane 134, Hsin Yi Rd., Section 3, **Taipei** (709-2000) 2 Chung Cheng 3rd Rd., 3rd Floor, **Kaohsiung** (224-0154)	None

Country	Risk Level	American Foreign Service	Canadian Representation
TADZHIKISTAN	III	Hotel Independence, 4th Floor, 105A Rudaki Prospect, **Dushanbe** (248-233)	Contact Russia
TANZANIA	III	36 Laibon Rd. (off Bagamoyo Rd.), **Dar-es-Salaam** (66010...15)	38 Mirambo St., **Dar-es-Salaam** (46000, 46011)
THAILAND	III	95 Wireless Rd., **Bangkok** (252-5040) Vidhyanond Rd., **Chiang Mai** (252-629) 9 Sadao Rd., **Songkhla** (321-441) 35/6 Supakitjanya Rd., **Udorn** (244-270)	Boonmitr Bldg., 11th Floor, 138 Silom Road, **Bangkok** (237-4126)
TOGO	III	Rue Pelletier Caventou & Rue Vauban, **Lome** (21-29-91...94)	Contact Ghana
TONGA	II	Contact Fiji	Contact Wellington, New Zealand
TRINIDAD AND TOBAGO	II	15 Queen's Park West, **Port-of-Spain** (622-6371)	1st. Floor, Huggins Building, 74 South Quay, **Port-of-Spain** (623-4770)
TUNISIA	III	144 Ave. de la Liberte, **Tunis** (782-566)	3 Rue du Senegal St., Place d' Afrique, **Tunis** 798-004, 796-577)
TURKEY	III	110 Ataturk Blvd., **Ankara** (426-5470) 104-108 Mesrutiyet Caddesi, Tepebasl, **Istanbul** (251-3602) Ataturk Caddesi, **Adana** (139-106)	Nenehatun Caddesi 75, Gaziosmanpasa, **Ankara** (436-1275...79) Buyukdere Cad. 107/3, Begun Han, Gayrettepe, **Istanbul** (172-5174)
TURKMENISTAN	III	Hotel Jubileniya, **Ashgabat** (24-49-25)	Contact Russia

Country	Risk Level	American Foreign Service	Canadian Representation
TUVALU	II	None	Contact Wellington, New Zealand
UGANDA	III	Parliament Ave., **Kampala** (259792/3/5)	Fifth St., Industrial Area, **Kampala** (25-81-41)
UKRAINE	II	Yuria Kotsubinskoho 10, **Kiev** (244-7354)	31 Yaroslaviv Val St., **Kiev** (131479)
UNITED ARAB EMIRATES	III	Al-Sudan St., **Abu Dhabi** (336-691) Dubai International Trade Center, **Dubai** (313-115) (Both: Saturday-Wednesday)	Contact Kuwait City, Kuwait
UNITED STATES OF AMERICA	I		501 Pennsylvania Ave., N.W., **Washington, D.C.** (202-682-1740) One CNN Center, South Tower, Ste. 400, **Atlanta** (404-577-6810) 3 Copley Pl., Ste 400, **Boston** (617-262-3760/7767/8562/3994) Suite 3000, 1 Marine Midland Center, **Buffalo** (716-852-1247) 2 Prudential Plaza, 180 N. Stetson Ave., Ste. 2400, **Chicago** (312-616-1860) Illuminating Bldg., Ste. 1008, 55 Public Square,**Cleveland** (216-771-0150) Suite 1700, St. Paul Place, 750 N. St. Paul St., **Dallas** (214-922-9806) 600 Renaissance Center, Ste. 1100, **Detroit** (313-567-2340)

Country	Risk Level	American Foreign Service	Canadian Representation
UNITED STATES OF AMERICA (Cont.)			300 S. Grand Ave., 10th Floor, **Los Angeles** (213-687-7432) 701-4th Ave. S., **Minneapolis** (612-333-4641) 1251 Ave. of the Americas, **New York** (212-768-2400) 50 Fremont St., Ste. 2100, **San Francisco** (415-495-6021) 412 Plaza 600, Sixth & Stewart, **Seattle** (206-443-1777)
URUGUAY	II	Calle Lauro Muller 1776, **Montevideo** (23-60-61)	18 de Julio 1263, **Montevideo** (91-24-59)
UZBEKISTAN	III	82 Chelanzarskaya, **Tashkent** (771-407)	Contact Russia
VANUATU	III	Contact Papua New Guinea	Contact Canberra, Australia
VENEZUELA	III	Avenida Francisco de Miranda and Avenida Principal de la Floresta, **Caracas** (285-3111/2222/2475) Edificio Banco Hipotecario del Zulia (BHZ), Calle 77 con Avenida 13, **Maracaibo** (84-253/4)	Edificio Torre Europa, 7th Floor, Avenida Francisco de Miranda, Campo Allegre, **Caracas** (951-6166..68)
VIETNAM	III	None	39 Nguyen Dinh Chieu St., **Hanoi** (42-65840/65845)
VIRGIN ISLANDS (BRITISH)	II	Contact Antigua and Barbuda	None

Country	Risk Level	American Foreign Service	Canadian Representation
VIRGIN ISLANDS (U.S.)	II	U.S. Territory	None
WESTERN SAMOA	II	John Williams Bldg., 5th Floor, Beach Road, Apia (21-631)	Contact Wellington, New Zealand
YEMEN ARAB REPUBLIC (NORTH YEMEN)	III	Dhahr Himyar Zone, Sheraton Hotel District, Sanaa (238-843/52) (Saturday-Wednesday)	Yemen Computer Co. Ltd. Bldg. 4, St. 11 off Haddah St., Sanaa; also contact Riyadh, Saudi Arabia
YEMEN, PEOPLE'S DEMOCRATIC REPUBLIC OF (SOUTH YEMEN)	III	None	None
ZAIRE	III	310 Ave. des Aviateurs, Kinshasa (21532, 21628)	17 Pumbu Ave. Kinshasa (6-0214)
ZAMBIA	III	Cor. Independence & United Nations Aves., Lusaka (228-595)	Barclays Bank North End Branch, Cairo Rd., Lusaka (22-88-11/12, 22-51-60, 22-85-81)
ZIMBABWE	III	172 Herbert Chitepo Ave., Harare (794-521)	45 Baines Ave., Harare (73-38-81...85)

Appendix C

IMMUNIZATIONS FOR TRAVELERS

This appendix contains general information about some of the more common immunizations which travelers might need to receive. Recommendations and requirements for immunizations are subject to frequent revision, because policies, prevailing opinions, and disease patterns are constantly changing and because medical practices are subject to change. Contact the CDC Traveler's Hotline (404-332-4559) or a travel health specialist for up-to-date information.

❖

CHOLERA vaccine is usually given in two doses, four weeks apart, to those visiting high-risk areas. Boosters may be given every six months. This vaccine is not very effective, but some nations may require a single dose prior to entry.

HAEMOPHILUS should be given to children between the ages of eighteen months and five years. It is administered as a single dose, and does not require a booster.

HEPATITIS A *(Immune globulin)* vaccine should be considered by those visiting high-risk areas. A single dose is usually given just prior to departure, and boosters are generally administered every four to six months.

HEPATITIS B vaccine also should be considered by those visiting high-risk areas, especially if sexual activity with local residents is anticipated. It is usually given in three doses, the first two separated by four weeks and the third six months later. Boosters are not necessary. People who have already had Hepatitis B have life-long immunity to the disease. This can be established by a blood test.

INFLUENZA immunization is advisable for those over sixty-five years of age and for others with chronic lung or heart disease. It is not recommended during the first three months of pregnancy. A single dose is injected, usually in the Fall, and annual boosters are recommended.

MEASLES/MUMPS/RUBELLA is a live vaccine. Everyone born after 1957 should probably receive this immunization, except for pregnant women and the immune-compromised. The Rubella vaccine is not recommended during the first four months of pregnancy and whenever the patient has a fever. A single dose of this multiple immunization is usually given to children. A booster is not necessary. Once you have had these diseases, you have life-long immunity.

MENINGOCOCCUS A single dose of meningococcus vaccine is advisable for those visiting areas of outbreak. This vaccine is not effective in young children. The appropriate timing of a booster has not been determined.

PERTUSSIS *(Whooping Cough)* vaccine is routinely given to children up to the age of seven. It is generally administered along with the immunization for Tetanus and Diphtheria. The pertussis vaccine is not recommended for pregnant women. Boosters are not required.

PLAGUE vaccine should be given to those visiting high-risk areas, but it is not advisable for pregnant women. Normally, three doses are given, two separated by a period of four weeks and a third three to six months later. Two boosters are usually given at six-month intervals, then every year or two thereafter.

PNEUMOCOCCUS vaccine should be given, in a single dose, to those over sixty-five years of age and to others with chronic lung or heart disease, a missing spleen, or sickle-cell disease. A booster is not required.

POLIO vaccine is administered in two forms. A doctor should help choose the form of the vaccine, the number of doses to be given, and the schedule of the doses.

The first form is an oral vaccine. This can be given to children up to the age of eighteen in three doses, the first two six to eight weeks apart and the third six or more weeks later.

A booster is advisable for adults who plan to travel to high-risk areas. This live vaccine should not be taken by pregnant women or those with impaired immune systems.

The second is a killed, injectable vaccine. Adults who have not received the oral version and those who are traveling to high-risk areas should generally receive three immunization doses, two initial doses six to eight weeks apart and a third six to twelve months later. Boosters are not normally required.

RABIES *(HDCV)* vaccine should be given to those visiting high-risk areas. Usually, two doses are given a week apart, and a third three weeks later. Boosters are recommended every two years. The antibody response should be checked after receiving the series.

TETANUS/DIPHTHERIA is a vaccination which most people in developed countries receive as children. Everyone should have had this immunization. It is administered in four doses, the first three at intervals of four to eight weeks and the fourth between six and twelve months later. A booster is advisable every ten years.

TYPHOID vaccine is available in oral and injectable forms. It should be given to anyone visiting high-risk areas, but it is not advisable for pregnant women. The oral vaccine, which has fewer side effects, is given in four doses, every second day, with a booster every five years. The injectable vaccine involves two inoculations, four weeks apart, and a booster every three years.

YELLOW FEVER is a live vaccine. A single dose should be given to those visiting high-risk areas, with boosters advisable every ten years. This vaccine should not be given to pregnant women, children under the age of nine months, immune-compromised individuals, or anyone allergic to eggs. Some nations may require a yellow fever vaccination prior to entry.

Appendix D

FOREIGN PHRASES

FOR HEALTH EMERGENCIES

If you need medical help in a country whose language you do not speak, the following foreign phrases may prove useful. If you are not certain of the pronunciation, simply point to the appropriate phrase. Phrases are provided in **English,** French, *German*, SPANISH, and *Italian*.

For other languages and for more complete listings of health and emergency phrases, refer to a traveler's dictionary, such as a Berlitz phrasebook, for the language in question.

I have a headache
> J'ai mal à la tête
>> *Ich habe Kopfschmerzen*
>>> TENGO DOLOR DE CABEZA
>>>> *Ho mal di testa*

I have a pain in my chest
> J'ai mal à la poitrine
>> *Ich habe Schmerzen in der Brust*
>>> TENGO DOLOR DE PECHO
>>>> *Ho un dolore al petto.*

I have a pain in the abdomen
> J'ai mal à l'abdomen
>> *Ich habe Bauchschmerzen*
>>> TENGO DOLOR DE BARRIGA
>>>> *Ho un dolore all' addome*

I have a cough
> J'ai la toux
>> *Ich habe Husten*
>>> TENGO TOS
>>>> *Ho una tosse.*

I feel nauseous
> J'ai la nausée
>> *Mir ist übel*
>>> TENGO NÁUSEAS
>>>> *Mi sento nauseato.*

I have an earache
> J'ai mal aux oreilles
>> *Ich habe Ohrenschmerzen*
>>> TENGO DOLOR DE ÓIDOS
>>>> *Ho mal d'orecchio*

My throat is sore
> J'ai mal à la gorge
>> *Mein Hals tut weh*
>>> ME DUELE LA GARGANTA
>>>> *Ho mal di gola*

I'm allergic to ...
> Je suis allergique à ...
>> *Ich bin allergisch gegen ...*
>>> TENGO ALERGIA A ...
>>>> *Sono allergico a ...*

I have a toothache
> J'ai mal aux dents
>> *Ich habe Zahnschmerzen*
>>> TENGO DOLOR DE MUELAS
>>>> *Ho mal di denti*

My blood type is ...
> Mon groupe sanuin est ...
>> *Meine Blutgruppe ist ...*
>>> MI GRUPO SANGUÍNEO ES ...
>>>> *Il mio gruppa sanguigno é ...*

I am a diabetic
Je suis diabétique
Ich bin Diabetiker
SOY DIABÉTICO
Sono diabetico/diabetica

I regularly take medication for ...
Je prends régulièrement des médicaments pour ...
Ich nehme regelmässig Medikamente gegen ...
ESTOY TOMANDO MEDICINAS PARA ...
Di solito prendo medicine pre ...

Can I continue traveling?
Puis-je continuer à voyager?
Kann ich meine Reise fortführen?
¿PUEDO CONTINUAR VIAJANDO?
Posso continuare a viaggiare?

Appendix E

SELECTED TRAVELERS' DISEASES

Chapter 3 discusses how to deal with common health problems and how to know when a problem is serious enough to require medical help. A number of the diseases which call for professional attention are described in this appendix. The risk of contracting some of these diseases is very low. These have been included for the sake of completeness or because they have been mentioned in the text. This appendix, however, is not an exhaustive listing of all the diseases or symptoms which you might encounter in your travels.

Use this appendix for reference only. The information presented here will provide you with some background information about selected diseases in the event that you need to receive medical treatment.

Do not attempt to self-diagnose or self-treat yourself on the basis of the information provided here. Many of these are potentially serious illnesses which require the professional experience of a trained physician to be diagnosed accurately and treated effectively.

The information presented here may also help you recognize the symptoms of a disorder which requires medical attention. This is particularly useful if you will be traveling in an area where there is a high risk of contracting one of these serious diseases. If you do become ill, recognizing the symptoms quickly can be helpful—and sometimes essential—in the treatment of the disease. The information presented here is not sufficient by itself to permit an accurate diagnosis, but it should give you a general idea of symptoms to watch out for. *Once again, only a doctor can diagnose these diseases accurately and verify the diagnosis..*

❖

AFRICAN SLEEPING SICKNESS *(African Trypanosomiasis)* Sleeping sickness is found in tropical Africa. It is caused by a protozoan, or trypanosome, transmitted by the bite of the tsetse fly. A small chancre, or sore, typically appears at the site of the bite a few days after the victim has been bitten. The sore becomes painful and hard at its center and the surrounding area becomes swollen. Fever, headache, rash, swollen lymph nodes, and mental changes usually follow. In the late stages of the disease, the victim becomes sleepy and lethargic, ultimately going into a coma and dying. If you are in tsetse fly area, get immediate medical attention at the first appearance of a suspicious sore. The drugs which are used to treat sleeping sickness are effective only in the early stages of the disease. Prevention begins with taking precautions against insect bites.

ANTHRAX Anthrax is found mostly in Haiti, Africa, the Middle East, and Asia. It is caused by contact with animals and animal products, including wool and leather, which contain bacterial spores. These spores may be infectious even after many years on the contaminated item. For example, goatskin craft products from Haiti have been banned in the United States because they have been found to be infected with anthrax. Rugs and wool products from the Middle East have caused anthrax when the spores were shaken out of them back home. Symptoms include an open sore with a red rim and a dark center. This is followed by headache, muscle aches, fever, nausea, and vomiting. If the bacterial spores are inhaled, they can cause a potentially fatal lung infection. Anthrax is treated with antibiotics. To prevent anthrax, avoid contact with infected animals and animal products in areas where anthrax is prevalent. If any symptoms appear after such contact, seek medical help. A vaccine is available if you know in advance that you will have extensive contact with potentially infected animals.

BRUCELLOSIS *(Undulant Fever)* Brucellosis is caused by bacteria transmitted through drinking unpasteurized milk from infected cows or goats and through contact with sick animals. It occurs worldwide. Its symptoms, which may begin anywhere from five days to months after exposure, include fatigue, loss of appetite, headache, and aches and pains. After a few days an intermittent (rising and falling) fever occurs, accompanied by chills and sweating. The symptoms will go away by themselves, but the disease remains present and the fever may recur. Medical treatment is required, even though the mortality rate is low. To prevent brucellosis, use only boiled or pasteurized dairy products (milk, cheese, yogurt, etc.) and avoid contact with animals that may be infected, especially if you have any open cuts or sores.

CHAGAS' DISEASE *(American Trypanosomiasis)* This disease, found in Mexico, South and Central America, is caused by a protozoan parasite, or trypanosome, transmitted by the bite of the reduviid, or 'kissing,' bug. This brown, oval bug, about an inch long, lives in thatched roofs and adobe walls. The painless purple swelling which appears at the site of the bite (usually on the face) is followed by fever, lymph node enlargement, diarrhea, and vomiting. The symptoms may go away if the body is able to eliminate the disease, but if Chagas' disease goes on untreated it can damage the heart many years later. The disease can only be cured in its early stages, so if you suspect that you have been bitten by an infected reduviid bug, see a doctor for testing right away. Prevent the disease by avoiding overnight stays in houses that may be infested with the bug, by spraying your rooms with insecticide, and by sleeping under netting.

CHOLERA Cholera is a serious intestinal disease caused by the toxin of *Vibrio cholerae* bacteria. It is transmitted through food or water that has been contaminated with feces. Epidemics of cholera have killed tens of thousands of people. In a recent outbreak of cholera in South America, many people became infected by eating uncooked contaminated fish. Symptoms include explosive, watery diarrhea along with vomiting, cramps, dehydration, and extreme weakness. Medical help and perhaps hospitalization are important to maintain adequate hydration, especially when both vomiting and diarrhea occur. The best protection against cholera is observing proper food and water precautions. A cholera vaccine is available. While it is only about fifty-percent effective, the vaccine may be advisable for those who will be traveling in areas off the normal tourist routes, where cholera is widespread.

CIGUATERA POISONING *(Fish Poisoning)* Fish poisoning is caused by a toxin produced by a dinoflagellate, a small marine organism eaten by many different kinds of reef fish, including barracuda, red snapper, sea bass, moray eel, and grouper. It is prevalent in the Caribbean and the tropical Pacific. Contamination in the fish is impossible to detect, and cooking does not destroy the toxin. Symptoms, which appear up to six hours and sometimes even weeks or months after eating contaminated meat, include numbness and tingling of the lips and tongue, nausea, watery diarrhea, cramps, and vomiting. Ciguatera symptoms may also include abnormal sensations, such as reversal of hot and cold. In some cases, potentially fatal respiratory failure may develop. There is no specific treatment for ciguatera poisoning. If you become ill after eating seafood, try to induce vomiting, drink plenty of fluids, and get medical help to treat the symptoms.

DENGUE FEVER *(Breakbone Fever)* Dengue fever is caused by a virus transmitted by a mosquito which bites during the day. It is found throughout the tropics. The disease is marked by two periods of fever. The first usually begins five to eight days after infection with the sudden onset of a high fever, chills, and muscle and joint pain. After two to four days, the fever goes down and is replaced by sweating. About twenty-four hours later, the fever reappears, typically accompanied by a bright red body rash and headache. Treatment, which is directed at relieving symptoms, includes rehydration and non-aspirin medication for pain and fever. (Aspirin can produce complications from bleeding). To prevent the disease, avoid mosquito bites during the daytime by using repellent and wearing long sleeves and pants.

DIPHTHERIA Diphtheria is a serious bacterial disease caused by the bacillus *Corynebacterium diphtheriae*. It is rare in developed countries, where immunizations and boosters are routinely administered. However, it is still a virulent and potentially fatal disease in many other parts of the world. Diphtheria is spread by touch or by air, and the bacillus can be carried by people who themselves are immune to the disorder. Symptoms include sore throat, fever, a gray, filmy coating over the tonsils and throat, enlarged lymph glands, and a rapid pulse. Diphtheria can lead to heart failure and paralysis even weeks after the initial exposure. Prevention is accomplished by vaccination. Treatment may include antibiotics, antitoxins, isolation, and occasionally a tracheotomy to ease breathing.

DYSENTERY Severe diarrhea with blood and mucus in the stools is known as dysentery. It can be caused by both amoebas and bacteria. *Amoebic* dysentery is marked by diarrhea and cramping with mucus and sometimes blood, but usually no fever. Stool analysis and medical treatment are necessary, because if it is not properly treated amoebic dysentery may cause liver abscess. *Bacillary* dysentery, caused by *Shigella* bacteria, may go away on its own after about a week. It is marked by watery diarrhea with blood or mucus, abdominal cramps, and usually a fever. A stool analysis will determine the cause of the illness. It can be life-threatening for children and people in weakened condition. Medical treatment consists of rehydration and antibiotics.

FILARIASIS This is actually a group of diseases found in the tropics and caused by roundworms transmitted by the bites of various species of mosquitoes. Symptoms, which may appear months after the bite, include fever, chills, headache, and swollen and painful lymph nodes. Repeated infections can lead to enlargement of body parts (*elephantiasis*). Filariasis is prevented by taking the usual precautions against mosquito bites. It can be treated effectively with antibiotics.

GIARDIASIS Giardiasis is an intestinal infection caused by the protozoan *Giardia lamblia*. It is transmitted throughout the world by the consumption of contaminated food or water, including untreated water in wilderness areas in the United States. Symptoms include yellow, foul smelling, frothy diarrhea without blood or mucus; gas and cramps; and abdominal discomfort. Some cases clear up by themselves. The victim can promote healing by drinking plenty of liquids, eating a good diet, and getting plenty of rest. Medical treatment includes the use of antibiotics.

HAEMOPHILUS *Haemophilus influenzae* is a common cause of meningitis (see meningococcal meningitis, below) and other, serious bacterial illnesses, such pneumonia. It is particularly dangerous for children under the age of five years.

Its symptoms may be flu-like, or they may reflect other conditions caused by the Haemophilus. Children between the ages of eighteen months and five years should have been routinely immunized against Haemophilus. Treatment includes the use of antibiotics.

HEPATITIS Hepatitis is a liver disease caused by viruses. Hepatitis A, or infectious hepatitis, is transmitted through contaminated water, shellfish, and improperly handled foods. Hepatitis B is transmitted through the exchange of blood, unsterilized needles (including tattoo and acupuncture needles), contaminated blood products, and through sexual activity. Hepatitis B is generally more serious, and its symptoms take longer to develop. Early symptoms of hepatitis are loss of appetite, fatigue, general malaise, and, among smokers, a lack of craving for cigarettes, followed by jaundice (yellowish coloration of the eyes and skin), dark urine, light-colored stools, fever, and headache. Medical treatment is required, although there is no specific cure. Resting, drinking plenty of fluids, and eating a good, high-protein diet are essential, as is avoiding alcohol and drugs, both of which are toxic to the liver. To avoid contaminating others, hepatitis patients should wash their hands carefully, refrain from handling food or sharing dishes and silverware, and abstain from sex. Once jaundice has set in, Hepatitis A generally ceases to be contagious. Immune serum globulin (gamma globulin) helps to prevent symptoms of hepatitis A, while hepatitis B vaccination helps protect those who are at high risk of exposure to hepatitis B.

INFLUENZA The 'flu' is a viral infection of the respiratory, nervous, or gastrointestinal system. It may be uncomfortable, but it is usually not fatal except among the very young, the elderly, and others with weakened or compromised immune systems. However, influenza can lead to serious infections, such as bronchitis or pneumonia. The flu is normally transmitted on airborne droplets coughed or sneezed by infected persons. Initial symptoms include, fever, chills, headache, muscle aches, fatigue, and weakness. These may be followed by a cough, chest pains, a sore throat, or a runny nose. Most of the time, the disease will clear up by itself in a week to ten days. Vaccination against influenza is a reasonably effective preventative, one which is recommended for pregnant women after the first trimester and for others at special risk. The treatment of influenza includes rest, pain-relievers, and plenty of liquids. Antibiotics have no effect on flu.

JAPANESE ENCEPHALITIS Japanese encephalitis is caused by a virus which is transmitted by mosquito bites. Epidemics occur in Asia during summer and fall, when the mosquito populations are highest. The disease produces no symptoms in most of the people it infects, but it can be fatal when symptoms do appear. These flu-like symptoms begin four to fourteen days after infection with fever, chills, aches and pains, etc. The disease can progress to drowsiness, lethargy, confusion, stiff neck, and in severe cases, to convulsions, paralysis, coma, and death. There is no specific treatment for Japanese encephalitis, but medical support is essential. A vaccine for preventing this disease is now available in a number of countries, including the United States.

LYME DISEASE Lyme disease is caused by a bacterial spirochete transmitted by tick bites. It is found worldwide and has become a significant health problem in the United States for hikers, campers, and others spending time in wooded areas. The first symptom is a painless round skin lesion, with a clear center and raised borders, at the site of the bite. This is followed by flu-like symptoms such as headache, stiff neck, chills, fever, joint pain, and fatigue. Symptoms may progress to arthritis, nerve problems, skin problems, heart problems, and muscle pains. Treatment with antibiotics is most effective in the early stages of the disease. Prevent Lyme disease by avoiding tick bites.

MALARIA Malaria is the most common infectious disease in the world today. It is transmitted by the bite of a female *Anopheles* mosquito infected with *Plasmodium*, a parasitic protozoan. Of the four varieties of this protozoan, *Plasmodium falciparum* is the most dangerous. The mosquito bites mainly at dusk and after dark, injecting the parasite into the blood stream. The parasite then migrates to the liver, where it multiplies. Some time later the parasites are released from the liver back into the blood stream. Symptoms appear when the parasite is free in the blood, anywhere from a single week to months after exposure. They include the sudden onset of fever, chills, and headache, followed by sweating. The symptoms subside and then recur in 2 or 3 days. Travelers visiting areas of malaria risk should take the usual precautions against mosquito bites and follow a preventive, anti-malaria drug regimen appropriate for the individual's health status and the local patterns of drug resistance. These same preventive drugs, as well as some others, are used to treat the disease once it has occurred. Diagnosis is made on the basis of microscopic examination of a blood smear. Recurrences of malaria are not uncommon. The blood-liver-blood cycle of malaria growth can repeat itself indefinitely, and some forms of the parasite can remain in the liver, causing relapses for years. Any recurrence of malaria symptoms after returning home should be treated with appropriate medication to prevent further relapses.

MEASLES This childhood disease is still widespread and potentially lethal in those parts of the world where measles vaccine is not routinely administered. It is caused by a virus that is spread through direct transfer and through the air. The first symptoms appear nine to eleven days after exposure. They include irritability, fever, runny nose, eyelid inflammation and swelling, light sensitivity, and cough. Two weeks after exposure, a rash begins on the face and spreads downward, and spots appear in the mouth. Usually the disease goes away by itself, but because it can have serious complications, the victim should be watched by a doctor. Travelers from the United States should receive measles vaccination before leaving home unless they have already had the disease.

MENINGOCOCCAL MENINGITIS Outbreaks of meningococcal meningitis are common in the tropics, especially in sub-Saharan Africa. Recent epidemics have occurred in Nepal, Kenya, and New Delhi, India. The disease comes on very quickly. Immediate diagnosis and medical treatment are essential because the consequences of meningococcal meningitis can be quite serious. It is transmitted when infected droplets are inhaled. Symptoms consist of a sudden onset of chills, fever, headache, vomiting, confusion, and sometimes a pinhead-size rash. The disease is diagnosed by examination of the spinal fluid. Treatment with appropriate antibiotics should begin as early as possible. A vaccine is available for people traveling to areas of meningitis epidemic.

MUMPS Mumps is caused by a virus transmitted in infected saliva and possibly urine. It is found worldwide, although vaccination has made it less of a threat in the United States. The main symptom is painful, swollen salivary glands, possibly accompanied by fever, sore throat, and perhaps other generalized inflammation. Mumps can produce serious complications—in adult males, for example, it may cause sterility. One case of mumps gives lifetime immunity. The next best protection is vaccination.

PERTUSSIS *(Whooping Cough)* This infectious disease is caused by bacteria that are inhaled on airborne droplets. The characteristic spasmodic cough and breathing difficulties develop after early symptoms such as sneezing, runny nose, cough, and fever. Whooping cough can be a serious disease among infants and young children, sometimes leading to potentially fatal pneumonia. Treatment is with antibiotics and hospitalization for coughing spasms. Children are routinely vaccinated against whooping cough in the United States with the DPT vaccine. Pertussis boosters should be up-to-date for children traveling abroad.

PLAGUE Plague is a bacterial infection that is transmitted from wild rodents to humans via flea bites. It is found in many parts of the world, including Africa, Southeast Asia, the Near East, South America, and the western United States, mainly in rural highlands. Symptoms of the disease appear suddenly one to five days after exposure. They include high fever, headache, chills, and the characteristic swollen lymph nodes, or buboes, for which bubonic plague is named. It is also called the black plague because the red hemorrhages it produces under the skin soon turn black and blue. The disease has a high mortality rate, but medical treatment with antibiotics reduces mortality significantly. Prevent exposure by avoiding contact with rodents and by using repellents to prevent flea bites. Plague vaccine might be appropriate for those visiting areas where there is a high risk of exposure to infected animals. The vaccine is not generally recommended for the ordinary traveler.

PNEUMOCOCCUS One of the most common forms of bacterial pneumonia is caused by *Streptococcus pneumoniae*, or pneumococcus. This lung inflammation can be contracted anywhere in the world, commonly as a secondary infection to a less serious illness. Symptoms include fever, chill, shortness of breath, chest pain, and a cough with yellow-green sputum or blood. Pneumococcus vaccine is available for the elderly and for others who are at risk from pneumonia. For most people, the disease will clear up in a couple of weeks. Advanced cases of pneumococcus, however, may require hospitalization.

POLIOMYELITIS Polio is transmitted through contaminated water or droplets from coughing. While most cases of polio are mild, the disease can destroy the central nervous system. Symptoms appear from three days to two weeks after exposure. They begin with a mild fever and can progress to muscle paralysis. There is no specific treatment for polio. It is routinely prevented by vaccination in developed countries. Polio immunizations should be up-to-date for anyone planning foreign travel.

RABIES Rabies is caused by a virus. This disease of the central nervous system is transmitted by bites of infected animals or by contact between infected saliva and open wounds. It can also be contracted from bat droppings. Rabies occurs worldwide, except for specific areas documented to be free of rabies. Among the animals which commonly carry the disease are dogs, cats, wolves, foxes, skunks, raccoons, bobcats, bats, and mongooses, but any animal biting without provocation should be suspected of being rabid. The first symptoms can appear from ten days to many months after exposure. These include pain or abnormal sensations at the site of the bite along with fever. Immediate medical care is essential, because the disease is generally fatal once symptoms appear. Treatment is with rabies vaccine and antiserum. People who are at high risk of exposure to rabid animals can be immunized in advance with human diploid cell rabies vaccine (HDCV).

RIVER BLINDNESS *(Onchocerciasis)* River blindness is caused by a tiny roundworm spread by the bite of blackflies which breed along fast-moving rivers in tropical areas of Africa and the New World. The onset of symptoms is delayed while the larvae of the worm penetrate the skin and mature. Symptoms include rash and itching and the formation of hard, scaly skin around the bite site. Characteristic of the disease is the formation of lumps under the skin. In the Americas, these lumps appear on the head and upper body, while in Africa they appear on the lower body and thighs. Drugs are available to treat the disease. It can be prevented by avoiding blackfly bites along rivers where the disease occurs.

RUBELLA *(German Measles)* Rubella is a viral disease with relatively mild effects for almost everyone except pregnant women. It is spread by airborne droplets propelled by sneezes or coughs. Symptoms, which appear two or three weeks after exposure, include a measles-like rash on the face, trunk, and arms, along with an occasional fever, runny nose, or swollen lymph nodes. It is a particular problem for women in their first four months of pregnancy, because the disease can cause serious birth defects, fetal abnormalities, and occasionally the death of the fetus. Rubella can be diagnosed only by a culture or blood test. There is no specific treatment except for rest. After natural immunity, the rubella vaccine is the most effective preventative. Non-immune women of child-bearing age who are not already pregnant should receive the vaccination.

SCHISTOSOMIASIS *(Bilharzia)* Schistosomiasis is a widespread disease caused by a parasitic flatworm which infests fresh water in tropical Africa and the Caribbean and in parts of Asia, South America, and the Middle East. The worm eggs enter the water through contaminated human feces or urine. They live in a snail host until they infect humans by burrowing through the skin and entering the bloodstream. A rash or irritation occurs at the site of entry, followed four to six weeks later by fever, chills, weakness, and a body rash. Advanced symptoms include frequent bloody diarrhea, enlarged abdominal organs, swollen lymph nodes, and serious organ involvement. Travelers in areas where the disease occurs should avoid all contact with fresh water, washing quickly and thoroughly after any accidental contact to prevent any worms present from entering the skin. Wherever schistosomiasis is a risk, even bath water should be boiled or chlorinated. Drugs are available to treat the disease, but avoiding possible exposure to contaminated water is the most important preventive measure.

TETANUS This deadly disease, caused by the bacterium *Clostridium tetani*, occurs worldwide. The bacteria live in human or animal feces and enter the body through wounds, especially gunshot, knife, and puncture wounds. The first symptom is stiffness of the jaw, which usually appears five to ten days after infection. This is followed by sore throat, headache, fever, muscle stiffness and spasm, and finally locking of the jaw, severe muscle spasms, and often death. Prevention is through immunization. Anyone who has not had a tetanus booster within the last five years should receive one upon suffering a serious wound. The tetanus inoculation should be up-to-date before foreign travel.

TRACHOMA This infectious disease is caused by the parasite *Chlamydia trachomatis*. A major cause of blindness in developing countries, it is spread from eye to eye through contact with dirty towels, hands, and flies. The disease starts with eye irritation and redness and can lead to scarring and eventual blindness. It is prevented by observing good hygiene and treated with antibiotics. Avoid contact with flies to prevent the disease.

TRICHINOSIS Trichinosis is caused by a roundworm that burrows into the intestines and muscles. It is spread through the consumption of contaminated pork and other meats, including bear and walrus, that have not been thoroughly cooked. The first symptoms of the disease—diarrhea, nausea, fever, and muscle pain—appear up to seven days after eating infected meat. Swollen eyelids often appear on the eleventh day, followed by chills, fever, muscle pain, and hemorrhages in the eyes and under the nails. Ultimately the disease can affect the heart, lungs, and nervous system. Trichinosis is treatable with medication, but it can be fatal if allowed to go untreated. Prevention includes avoiding the consumption of pork and other meats which have not been thoroughly cooked.

TUBERCULOSIS Tuberculosis (TB) is an infection caused by the bacteria *Mycobacterium tuberculosis* or *Mycobacterium bovis*. It is contracted by inhaling infected droplets and by consuming unpasteurized milk or dairy products. Tuberculosis is found worldwide and is even on the increase in many countries. The disease may not appear until a year after contact. The symptoms include weight loss, fever, night sweats, and bloody cough. Tuberculosis usually infects the lungs, but it can spread to other parts of the body and cause serious neurological damage and other problems. TB may be diagnosed with a chest x-ray. Travelers who plan to visit areas of high exposure risk should have TB skin tests before departing and follow-up tests after returning home to determine whether they have been exposed to the disease. Drugs are available to treat those who have been exposed to TB.

TYPHOID FEVER Typhoid is a disease caused by the bacteria *Salmonella typhi*, which is transmitted through contaminated water and food and often by infected food handlers. The disease begins like a cold or flu, with headache, sore throat, and a steadily rising fever which is accompanied by relatively slow pulse. A pulse that slows down while the fever rises is, in fact, a plausible sign of typhoid. During the second week of the illness, a high fever, a relatively slow pulse, and perhaps a few pink spots on the body, gradually progress to weakness, delirium, trembling, and dehydration. The disease can continue for as long as eight weeks. Medical treatment and possibly hospitalization are required. Treatment includes antibiotics and the maintenance of adequate hydration. Typhoid vaccine provides partial protection against the disease for people who will be traveling or staying where standards of hygiene and sanitation are poor. The best protection against the disease is to observe water and food precautions scrupulously.

TYPHUS Typhus is a disease is caused by bacteria-like organisms called *rickettsiae*. It is similar to typhoid, but it is transmitted through the bites of rat fleas, lice, mites, and ticks. Typhus occurs worldwide, most often in cool upland areas. It starts out like a bad cold and progresses after a week or more to chills, cough, headache, and muscle and chest pain, with a rash on the chest and abdomen. The fever may last for two weeks or more. Treatment is with antibiotics. Typhus vaccine is rarely required in the United States, because the more serious form of the disease has not been a problem for American travelers for many years. The best means of prevention is to maintain good hygiene, to avoid lice, and to use insecticide and repellents to ward off insect bites.

YELLOW FEVER Yellow fever is caused by a virus transmitted by mosquitos. It occurs in Africa and in Central and South America. Symptoms appear about two weeks after exposure with the sudden onset of a high fever and a rapid pulse which slows by the second day. The symptoms subside, but the period of remission is followed by fever, hemorrhaging, vomiting of black blood, jaundice (yellowness of eyes and skin), confusion, and delirium. There is no specific medical treatment for yellow fever except for maintaining hydration and keeping the fever down. The disease is prevented by yellow fever vaccine and by taking precautions against mos-

quito bites. Yellow fever vaccination is required for entry into
many countries. Anyone traveling to an area of yellow fever
risk should consider having the vaccination. However, some
people, including pregnant women and young infants, should
not receive this vaccine. They should consider avoiding areas
where the yellow fever risk is high.

Index

Order form

Please send me a full-sized set of forms and worksheets from *The Travel Health™ Clinic Pocket Guide To Healthy Travel* for my personal use.

This *Forms Package* includes reproducible copies of the *Trip Planning Worksheet*, the *Country Worksheet*, the *Medical Kit Checklist*, the *Medical Document Checklist*, and the *Emergency Information Checklist*.

I am enclosing a check for **$2.00** to cover handling and first-class postage.

Name	_____
Address	_____
	_____
City, State	_____
Zip	_____

SILVERCAT
San Diego, California

Silvercat Publications
4070 Goldfinch St., Suite C
San Diego, CA 92103-1865

(Please allow 4 weeks for delivery)